# YORK HANDBOOKS

GENERAL EDITOR:
Professor A.N. Jeffares
(*University of Stirling*)

# STUDYING JANE AUSTEN

## Ian Milligan
MA   M ED (GLASGOW)
*Lecturer in English,*
*University of Stirling*

LONGMAN
YORK PRESS

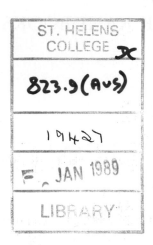
YORK PRESS
Immeuble Esseily, Place Riad Solh, Beirut.

LONGMAN GROUP UK LIMITED
Longman House, Burnt Mill, Harlow,
Essex CM20 2JE, England
and Associated Companies throughout the World.

First published 1988

ISBN 0-582-79282-7

Produced by Longman Group (FE) Ltd
Printed in Hong Kong

# Contents

# Preface

Reading the novels of Jane Austen can be one of the greatest pleasures that English fiction provides, but many students do not find them easy. Changes in manners, customs and language, not to mention the material circumstances of life, may obscure the similarities between the interests and attitudes of people of her day and ours. Yet, underneath these superficial differences, the questions which arise about human behaviour have hardly changed. Jane Austen's early fiction, written when she was in her 'teens, made outrageous fun of the way contemporary novelists represented the lives of people living then. As a mature writer, she used her imagination to devise new ways of presenting the lives of young people, so that their hopes, confusions, follies and virtues might be recorded vividly and sympathetically, and she used her sharp wit to pierce the pretentiousness, snobbery and complacency of the society in which they grew up.

This book aims to introduce new readers to these great works by establishing as clearly as possible the real issues which lie beneath the talk and actions of the novels; it offers comment on their themes, their language and the ironic, but deeply concerned, light in which the author views her characters; it considers the relationships between the novels and discusses the development of Jane Austen's distinctive novelistic techniques. Its purpose will be served if new readers of Jane Austen's novels enjoy their work and understand them better, learning in the process, perhaps, a new respect for 'the common feelings of common life'. I should like to thank Professor A.N. Jeffares for his support and encouragement, the publishers for their patience, and my wife for the pleasure she has taken in talking about Jane Austen.

# Chapter 1

# Introduction

## The life of Jane Austen

Jane Austen has come to be recognised as one of the greatest of English novelists. She was born in 1775, the sixth of a family of eight children, in a small village called Steventon, in Hampshire, a prosperous and essentially agricultural county of southern England. Both her parents were educated, intelligent and lively people, who came of established families of good social standing. Her father was a clergyman, who educated a few pupils along with his sons in his own home. Although he was not a rich man, he had wealthy relations who helped him and his family. One of Jane's brothers, indeed, was adopted and brought up as the heir to a great estate, and Jane spent the last six years of her life in a small house on his estate. She was part of a large, complicated network of family relationships that gave her personal experience of the life and manners of upper-middle-class families in the last years of the reign of George the Third. The Austens did not have close social relationships with the great landed families of the county, but they were established members of the local gentry. Jane Austen's father was not a poor country parson; he aimed to be a scholar and a gentleman. The reader of her novels is never allowed to forget the fine gradations of class distinction in English life at this time. Although she never married, she was deeply attached to her parents, to her sister, to her brothers and their families. She devoted much time and attention to their welfare, as her letters to them show. She was alert to all the small details of daily living — the interests, attachments, expectations, pleasures and disappointments, as well as the whims and passing fashions, which form the life of a large, active and loving family. Concern for others was a fundamental aspect of her character, though she saw them with a sharp eye and sometimes spoke of them with as sharp a tongue.

When she was seven years of age, Jane was sent away to school for five years with her elder sister, but perhaps it was in her father's library that her real education took place. She clearly enjoyed social life at Steventon; her letters record her friendships with the families of the small landowners of the neighbourhood; we hear of dances, social gatherings, flirtations. There were private theatrical performances in her father's barn, for which she wrote material, and her early works were written for reading aloud to the family. We know she read widely in the histories, novels, essays and sermons of the time. By the age of twenty-two she had completed her first novel and her father tried unsuccessfully to find a publisher for it. In 1803 a second attempt was made and an early version of *Northanger Abbey* was sold to a publisher, though it never appeared.

In 1801 Mr Austen retired from Steventon and took the family to Bath. The next eight years were not happy. Jane Austen may have felt uprooted; she had no great love for the bustle of town life. Her father died in 1805, leaving his widow with little money. She and her daughters moved about, then settled in Southampton with one of Jane's sailor brothers. In 1808 Jane's brother, Edward, now owner of the estate which he had been brought up to inherit, offered them a cottage near his great house at Chawton. Restored to the countryside which she loved and with much closer contact with her brothers and their families, Jane Austen began to write again. At Chawton her last three completed novels, *Mansfield Park* (1814), *Emma* (1815) and *Persuasion* (1818) were written and *Sense and Sensibility* (1811) and *Pride and Prejudice* (1813), which had both been written before she left Steventon, were revised and published. In 1817 she died prematurely of a wasting disease, and the sense of loss which the family suffered is movingly recorded in the *Memoir* (1870) written long afterwards by her nephew. Shortly after her death, *Northanger Abbey* and *Persuasion* were published together in four volumes (1818).

# Studying Jane Austen

## 1  What to study

The student's first aim will be to study the six completed novels published between the years 1811 and 1818, but it may not be easy to decide in which order they should be read. Expert opinion, based upon a note left by Jane Austen's sister, Cassandra, believes that *Elinor and Marianne*, an early form of *Sense and Sensibility*, was written in 1795 in the form of a series of letters and that the first version of *Pride and Prejudice*, entitled *First Impressions*, was begun in 1796 and finished by August of the following year. It has been suggested that in a revision of *Elinor and Marianne*, undertaken in 1797, the letter form was discarded. In the same year Jane's father wrote to a London publisher, offering him *First Impressions*, but the offer was refused. In 1797–8, *Susan*, which was the first title of *Northanger Abbey*, was written; in 1803 it was sold to a publisher, but was never published. In 1809 Jane Austen tried to retrieve the manuscript from the publisher so that she could offer it elsewhere, but he had paid £10 for it and he wanted it bought back at the same price. It was not until she settled with her mother and sister at Chawton Cottage that there were further thoughts of publication, and in 1811 *Sense and Sensibility* was published anonymously by a London publisher. *Pride and Prejudice* followed in January

1813, and in June of that year *Mansfield Park*, which she had began to write in 1811, was finished. She started to write *Emma* in 1814, and *Persuasion* in 1815.

Scholars disagree about how much her first published novels were revised before publication. It had generally been assumed that *Sense and Sensibility* and *Pride and Prejudice* were extensively revised in the period 1809 to 1810, but it has been argued that *Pride and Prejudice* received its major revision in 1802-3 and was only lightly revised before it was sent to the publisher after the success of *Sense and Sensibility*. In this Handbook, the novels are analysed in order of their publication, with the exception of *Northanger Abbey*, which though not published until 1818, is placed first. It is surely an early work which still bears evidence of Jane Austen's gift for literary parody which she displayed in all the writing of her girlhood and adolescent years.

## 2 Themes

The central subject-matter of Jane Austen's novels is the choice of a suitable marriage partner. Some argue that she was mistaken in stopping at the point when the choice had been made, thus neglecting to explore the problems of marriage itself. However, she would not have wished to write about matters outside her own experience, though all of her novels contain examples of less than satisfactory marriages where early idealism had disappeared along with the affections which brought them about. Jane Austen's main field of interest is courtship, because it is a process by which people gain knowledge of themselves and others in a peculiarly intimate way. In *Pride and Prejudice*, for example, she dwells on the way in which additional factual knowledge can change one character's understanding of another. Elizabeth Bennet's stereotyped picture of Darcy is shown to be inadequate when she becomes fully aware of his personal history. In the same way, her heroines' romantic idealisations of Willoughby in *Sense and Sensibility* and of Wickham in *Pride and Prejudice* are shown to be mistaken in fact, and are based more on sexual fantasy than on worth of character.

If knowing others depends on the gradual elimination of factual error, judging them is a more subtle process. How are we to estimate qualities such as intelligence, wit, good-humour, toleration and good taste? *Mansfield Park* offers, in Fanny Price, a character whose superiority of character soon becomes evident. From the less than perfect examples of those around her — or from some mysterious inner source of insight — she infers principles of behaviour which have a consistency and a degree of excellence superior to those of her more privileged cousins and even to those of her uncle himself. Fanny assumes that absolute standards of goodness exist and tries to shape her own behaviour in accordance with them. If we ask of what these standards consist, we must include honesty, breadth of vision, consistency and good-will. If her judgment of others by these standards appears to lay her open to charges of priggishness, we must admit that there is nothing narrowly censorious about her. The impersonality of her moral vision is established by contrast with the self-centredness of almost all of her companions. Many of her beliefs cause her considerable suffering, but she appears to believe that action based on principle is preferable to action based on self-interest or on a calculation of future benefit. We are invited to share Fanny's view of her situation and to consider how far her judgments are justified.

In *Emma* the themes of knowledge and judgment are combined. The correction of Emma's understanding of others goes hand in hand with her discovery of standards by which she may best govern her own life. It may appear to the reader that in her last two novels Jane Austen modifies her own values, finding a place for qualities which she had earlier treated with caution.

Again and again—but most poignantly in her last published novel, *Persuasion*—Jane Austen returns to the theme of feeling, that reservoir of intuitions, which may mislead, but for which there is no external substitute. It is only by being in touch with their feelings that her heroines can escape the bondage of subservience to imperfect social forms, to the domination of others or to inappropriate notions of duty. But what constitutes a correct judgment of these complex issues is the most testing question which each of them has to face.

## 3 Techniques

One of the main interests in studying Jane Austen is to follow the development of her fictional techniques, in particular her control of narrative and her ability to create character. When she began to write fiction as a young girl, she produced parodies of the kind of fiction then in fashion. The last vestiges of this style of writing can be seen in *Northanger Abbey* and in some of the speeches of Marianne in *Sense and Sensibility* and of Lady Catherine in *Pride and Prejudice*. Out of her parodies of current romantic fiction, she began to find ways of producing a closer representation of the lives of a selection of the people of her own time, and then to find ways of producing formal structures which would be adequate vehicles for her themes. In *Pride and Prejudice*, for example, verisimilitude and the amplitude of local detail are given more attention than in later novels where her main concern is that incidents should be grouped in patterns which most successfully illuminate underlying themes.

One of her principal methods of story-telling is the use of discovery. As in the modern detective-story, information is deliberately withheld (both from the principal character and from the reader) which must then be supplied in a plausible way. In *Pride and Prejudice*, a letter from Darcy himself supplies the first authentic account of his dealings with Wickham, while later in the novel the housekeeper of Pemberley supplies further details about these two men whom she knew as boys. Studying the novels in succession gives the reader an opportunity to see how Jane Austen develops her skill in handling the machinery of her plots, gradually dispensing with characters whose only function is to support the actions of others, and producing sequences of incidents which have their own unobtrusive rhythm. One of the special skills she develops is the management of dialogue whereby speech and the bodily gestures which accompany it become essential to the action of the novel, so that opinion, attitude and sentiment become forces which shape the plot. It is through speech, too, that she develops character, finding language which expresses the smart but heartless repartee of Mary Crawford (in *Mansfield Park*), the unstructured associative outpourings of Miss Bates and the suburban fantasies of Mrs Elton (both in *Emma*).

## 4 The aims of this book

This Handbook is meant to be practical, but its aims are limited. It is not meant to offer information about Jane Austen, though some biographical information is given. It is intended for students who want to extend their study of individual works by Jane Austen to a consideration of several of her novels or of her work as a whole. It has in mind the reader who may be preparing for an examination or an essay or a longer piece of work, who wants either an introduction to the six major novels or a reminder of their salient features. The chapters on the novels aim to provide a combination of summary and critical discussion which will throw light on the shape and character, the themes and techniques of each novel, while suggesting the features of substance and style which unite them. Readers will be interested to explore the developments in Jane Austen's art and to consider the artistic problems she appears to set herself and the means she devises to solve them.

# Chapter 2

# *Northanger Abbey*:
## the perils of fantasy

## Introduction

According to a memorandum by Jane Austen's sister, Cassandra, *Northanger Abbey* was originally written about the years 1798–9. It was bought by the London publishing house of Crosby and Co in 1803, when it was called *Susan*. Crosby and Co did not publish it, however, and it was repurchased in 1816 and published together with *Persuasion* in December 1818, five months after the author's death. In its first edition *Northanger Abbey* was published in two volumes: Volume One comprised Chapters 1–15; Volume Two, Chapters 16–31.

## Commentary

### Volume One *(Chapters 1–15)*

The first thing to be aware of in reading *Northanger Abbey* is its tone, in particular the tone of the narrative. Much of the novel is written in the spirit of burlesque which appears to be the driving force of Jane Austen's juvenile pieces, and which can occasionally be seen in her letters. What makes *Northanger Abbey* especially interesting is that it shows how the author is beginning to develop the technical means to present situations which are closer to 'the common feelings of common life' (Chapter 2) than those dealt with in the romantic novels and plays she loved to parody when she was young.

The first pages of the novel are written in the devastatingly brisk style which we have come to associate with the young Jane Austen. As it develops we notice the straight-faced extravagance which characterises her youthful parodies of sentimental fiction; consider the description of Catherine Morland and her family in Chapter 1:

> Her mother was a woman of useful plain sense, with a good temper, and, what is more remarkable, with a good constitution. She had three sons before Catherine was born; and instead of dying in bringing the latter into the world, as any body might expect, she still lived on — lived

on to have six children more—to see them growing up around her, and to enjoy excellent health herself. A family of ten children will always be called a fine family, where there are heads and arms and legs enough for the number; but the Morlands had little other right to the word, for they were in general very plain, and Catherine, for many years of her life, as plain as any. She had a thin awkward figure, a sallow skin without colour, dark lank hair, and strong features—so much for her person;— and not less unpropitious for heroism seemed her mind.

It might be difficult to suppose that any central character could recover from this unpromising introduction. Of course, we are aware that much of the irony is directed against the conventions associated with sentimental fiction—that heroines should be born into exceptional circumstances and be of outstanding beauty and intelligence—but what we are most aware of is the ruthless cleverness of the narrator. The writer of a sentence such as, 'A family of ten children will always be called a fine family, where there are heads and arms and legs enough for the number' is aware of her own wit: the more we admire its deftness, the less seriously can we take the people to whom it refers. The same can be said for the decisive 'so much for her person' which relegates Catherine to the ranks of the ordinary. But it gradually becomes apparent that Jane Austen means to be the champion of this very ordinariness. Her aim is to starve her readers' expectations of the extraordinary and to find an interest in the 'common feelings of com- mon life'. Catherine's first social appearance in the ball-room is an exhausting confirmation of her own unimportance, but she leaves it, con- tent to have had some notice taken of her, even if she has in point of fact found no friends.

Having vigorously deflated her heroine in the opening chapters of the novel, Jane Austen prepares to take her seriously. She introduces Cathe- rine to a hero in Henry Tilney, who not only continues the demystification of romance by mocking the social conventions of Bath, but is himself scarcely in the heroic mould. The interest he professes in muslins—an interest learned from his sister—almost prompts Catherine to call him strange, but it is a strangeness which intrigues her. By the end of their first meeting in Chapter 3, Catherine is sufficiently interested in him to express (to herself) a judgment on his character:

> [She] feared, as she listened to their discourse, that he indulged himself a little too much with the foibles of others—'What are you thinking of so earnestly?' said he, as they walked back to the ball-room;—'not of your partner, I hope, for, by that shake of the head, your meditations are not satisfactory'.
> Catherine coloured, and said, 'I was not thinking of any thing!'
> 'That is artful and deep, to be sure; but I had rather be told at once that you will not tell me.'

Well, then, I will not!

'Thank you; for now we shall soon be acquainted, as I am authorized to tease you on this subject whenever we meet, and nothing in the world advances intimacy so much!'

Henry Tilney now speaks to Catherine with the ironic raillery which was the mark of the narrator in the first chapter of the novel, but the narrator's attitude to Catherine has changed. Catherine is capable of thinking about character and in particular about Henry Tilney's habit of making ironic — and, therefore, superior — remarks about other people. She can give the appearance of thinking earnestly; she is prudent enough to conceal her thoughts, but she is honest and direct enough to admit, when challenged, that she is doing so. We have been guided by the narrative to discount Catherine as a romantic heroine only to find ourselves persuaded to respect her as a young woman of perfectly normal complexity.

It is not unusual in life that a newly-made friend should temporarily disappear and, in just such a provokingly normal way, so does Henry Tilney, leaving Catherine to watch the undifferentiated fashionable crowd passing her by. His place is taken by the Thorpe family, the eldest daughter of which, Isabella, has the looks, the manners and the aspirations of a romantic heroine. The connection between Catherine and Isabella is reinforced by the connection which has already been made at Oxford between their brothers. Jane Austen loses no time in displaying the differences in their character by involving them in animated conversation about the novels they have read.

The contrast between the girls is soon established: Isabella, the older and more assured of the two, quickly takes the lead. It is she who has introduced Catherine to the 'horrid' novels of Gothic romance, which she claims to enjoy. But it is soon clear that Isabella is more interested in what she wears than in what she reads, and that her overriding interest is in young men. Indeed, for Isabella, novels may be 'horrid' in quite another sense than the Gothic. A novel Catherine's mother has read and admired (a favourite novel of Jane Austen's, *Sir Charles Grandison* by Samuel Richardson (1689–1761)) is declared 'horrid' because in Isabella's view it is unreadable. Catherine's fascination with the novel she is reading is quickly brushed aside when Isabella fancies she is being noticed by 'two odious young men':

'For Heaven's sake! Let us move away from this end of the room. Do you know, there are two odious young men who have been staring at me this half hour. They really put me quite out of countenance. Let us go and look at the arrivals. They will hardly follow us there.'

Away they walked to the book; and while Isabella examined the names, it was Catherine's employment to watch the proceedings of these alarming young men.

'They are not coming this way, are they? I hope they are not so impertinent as to follow us. Pray let me know if they are coming. I am determined I will not look up.'

In a few moments Catherine, with unaffected pleasure, assured her that she need not be longer uneasy, as the gentlemen had just left the Pump-room.

'And which way are they gone?' said Isabella, turning hastily round. 'One was a very good-looking young man'.

'They went towards the churchyard.'

'Well, I am amazingly glad I have got rid of them! And now, what say you to going to Edgar's Buildings with me, and looking at my new hat? You said you should like to see it.'

Catherine readily agreed. 'Only,' she added, 'perhaps we may over-take the two young men.'

'Oh! never mind that. If we make haste, we shall pass by them pre-sently, and I am dying to shew you my hat.'

'But if we only wait a few minutes, there will be no danger of our see-ing them at all!' (*Chapter 6*)

In this scene Catherine's is the voice of innocent reasonableness; young men as a class do not have for her the potent fascination which they exert over Isabella. Isabella feels their fascination but does not honestly confront her feelings. She dissembles, and perhaps even deceives herself about what she feels. Although the words 'with unaffected pleasure' demonstrate that Catherine now has the author's sympathy and approbation, the passage is almost wholly dramatised. We are left to infer that Isabella has instructed Catherine to tell her what the young men are doing, while the phrase 'the proceedings of these alarming young men' carries a hint that Catherine may accept this as a true description of them, as well as a signal that the narrator does not expect us to believe it. Isabella's 'turning hastily round' suggests that she does not want to lose sight of them, and everything that she subsequently says reinforces her strong desire to pursue them without pub-licly admitting that she is doing so. As the two girls 'set off immediately as fast as they could walk, in pursuit of the two young men', they are followed by the smiling, undeceived eye of the narrator.

The opening of Chapter 7 cements the relationship between the author/narrator and her readers; whereas at the beginning of the novel we were people who might expect a heroine to be exceptional to the point of imbe-cility, now we are likely to be 'acquainted with Bath' and 'to remember the difficulties of crossing Cheap-street' at 'the archway, opposite Union-passage'. Having established her relationship with her readers and with her characters, Jane Austen begins to work out the consequences of the charac-ters and circumstances she has posited as the foundation of her story. The absence of Henry Tilney, followed by the arrival of two readily available young men, is sufficient to generate a complex narrative. Isabella has already made clear her interest in Catherine's brother, though Catherine is deaf to hints she drops. She leads him off, though not without several backward glances at the young men she was originally pursuing. John Thorpe and Isabella are quickly exposed as unsatisfactory friends. John Thorpe

> . . . was a stout young man of middling height, who, with a plain face and ungraceful form, seemed fearful of being too handsome unless he wore the dress of a groom, and too much like a gentleman unless he were easy where he ought to be civil and impudent where he might be allowed to be easy. (*Chapter 7*)

Jane Austen presents him as someone who is foolishly indecorous, unable through personal vanity to be an unoffending member of his own class. Isabella's vanity, on the other hand, is more straightforward: nothing shakes her satisfaction with herself.

In her innocence and youth, urged by her brother and by the supporting opinions of her friends, Catherine might well take the Thorpes for friends. As it is, she has absorbed the literary taste of Isabella, even if John Thorpe has shown that even by the minimal standards of the Gothic novels, his taste in reading is defective. To test the value of the Thorpes, Jane Austen re-introduces Henry Tilney supported now by a sister whose air,

> . . . though it had not all the decided pretension, the resolute stilishness of Miss Thorpe's, had more real elegance. Her manners shewed good sense and good breeding; they were neither shy, nor affectedly open . . . (*Chapter 8*)

Miss Tilney strikes the mean that John Thorpe fails to achieve and her behaviour is directly contrasted with what we know of Isabella. The key word 'elegance' carries with it a sense of appropriateness and discrimination; it refers to character rather than appearance, refinement rather than ostentation. Miss Tilney's 'good sense' and 'good breeding' are qualities which are qualified by no hint of irony. She sets a standard which the narrator commends to us without reservation, though Catherine's immediate interest is in her appearance and her relationship to Henry Tilney.

By contrast, Isabella's manner is arch and disingenuous: it becomes obvious that what she says she wants is what she does not want, and that what she feels is quite at variance with what she says. While she wants to appear to adhere to the 'rules' — of the dance or of broader social custom — she more particularly wants to do as she likes. In particular, she wants to attach herself to James Morland. Her mother shares her complacency: both her children are agreeable in her eyes — even the egregious John Thorpe.

Very soon, the action of the novel depends on Catherine's interest in Henry Tilney. Of course, she cannot hope to approach him directly: only through his sister does she have a chance of making contact with him. A major obstacle to her barely acknowledged aim is the unwelcome attention of John Thorpe, who is too stupidly immodest to suspect that she may be interested in anyone but him. When he arrives to whisk her off on a drive, she appeals in vain (by decently veiled hints) to Mrs Allen to save her. Surrounded by stupidity, indifferent selfishness and greed, she finds that her new friends only want to use her: Isabella's interest in her is shallowly conventional; John Thorpe believes that Mr Allen might make her rich. John Thorpe lives by exaggeration: he exaggerates the danger of driving just as he exaggerates his driving skill; he exaggerates the quality of his wine and how much of it he drinks. He exaggerates the merits of his own carriage and the dangerous insufficiency of the one James Morland is driving. Catherine is wholly unused to such verbal inconsistency:

> . . . she had not been brought up to understand the propensities of a rattle, nor to know to how many idle assertions and impudent falsehoods the excess of vanity will lead. Her own family were plain matter-of-fact people who seldom aimed at wit of any kind . . . (*Chapter 9*)

It is a paradox of Jane Austen's art that, with the sharpest and wittiest eye and tongue, she has the clearest insight into the damage such wit may do. Here, the narrator does not hesitate to express a preference for simplicity and decorum which the wit of the novel itself scarcely exemplifies. Mr and Mrs Morland may be reference points for correct behaviour but the novelist's interest focuses on their daughter's attempts to distinguish truth from falsehood and fact from fantasy, 'wit' from good sense. In these tasks quick-wittedness and a capacity for criticism and reflection do not come amiss: Catherine Morland has left behind the traditional order of her parents' village; she needs all her intelligence to survive. She soon learns that John Thorpe's habit of verbal extravagance is inseparably connected with his inflated self-esteem.

It is comparatively easy for her to dislike John Thorpe: the incompatibility of their interests allows her to judge him more objectively. It is more difficult for her to come to terms with Isabella: they are of an age; they both have a perfectly reasonable interest in romantic fiction and in young men, but Catherine has to learn that even where interests overlap, there are distinctions of quality to be made. For a moment the close identification which Jane Austen has achieved between her narrator and her principal character is relaxed, and we become aware of three levels on which the narrative operates: the lowest is the discourse of those characters who are oblivious of, or indifferent to, their own ignorance or dishonesty; the highest is the level of the narrative commentary, which alerts the reader to the hypocrisy and self-deception of those characters on the lowest level; finally there is the discourse of Catherine herself who has not yet attained the knowledge of the world and the command of the nuances of language, social conventions and moral truth which the narrator possesses and believes the reader to share.

The paragraph in Chapter 9 beginning, 'When they arrived at Mrs

Allen's door . . . ' offers an example of these varied voices. Initially, the principal voice is Isabella's, but the author keeps it under control by using the technique of *free indirect speech*. This offers a version of the speech — or, more often, the thoughts — of a character, transposed into the third person without any marker, such as 'she thought' or 'she said', to distinguish the reporter's point of view. Part of the reason for using this technique is to leave the reported material open to the judgment of the reader. The author withdraws from the position of commentator and leaves it to the reader to assess what the character says or thinks. Here the words and inflections are Isabella's, but they have been put into the past tense and the third person without completely losing the immediacy of direct speech. By slightly distancing what Isabella is saying in this way, Jane Austen can link Isabella's words more closely to the comments of the narrator. In the following passage, for example, 'Past three o'clock' are Isabella's own words, directly given. What follows is a report of what she says which is altered so slightly from what she must have said that the tone and accent of her sentences are perfectly preserved:

> . . . it was inconceivable, incredible, impossible! and she would neither believe her own watch, nor her brother's, nor the servant's; she would believe no assurance of it founded on reason or reality, till Morland produced his watch, and ascertained the fact; to have doubted a moment longer *then*, would have been equally inconceivable, incredible, and impossible . . . (*Chapter 9*)

The crescendo of exclamatory unbelief in simple fact, characteristic of Isabella, is quietly punctured by the narrator's reference to 'reason' and 'fact'. But Jane Austen makes it perfectly clear that it is not the fact of the matter which convinces Isabella, but the authority of the man with whom she has fallen in love and whom she wishes to impress with her devotion. The pendulum of Isabella's opinion depends on exaggerated and unexamined feeling; it owes nothing to 'reason' and 'fact'.

Now that the essential elements of her novel have been laid down, Jane Austen is content to allow its shape to be determined by the rhythm of social life of Bath. The evening at the ball is succeeded by one at the theatre where Catherine suffers more of Isabella's pointless chatter and tasteless innuendoes about her relationship with James Morland. Whether at the theatre or at the Pump Room, Catherine is obliged to be a listener only to Isabella's flirting with James. A chance meeting with Miss Tilney allows Jane Austen to display Catherine's naiveté, since she cannot disguise her keen interest in Henry Tilney's whereabouts and her eager wish to see him again. At the dance next evening her only anxiety is that John Thorpe may ask her to dance before Henry Tilney has a chance to do so. Jane Austen now feels sure enough of her reader's sympathy to say:

Every young lady may feel for my heroine in this critical moment, for every young lady has at some time or other known the same agitation. All have been, or at least all have believed themselves to be, in danger from the pursuit of some one whom they wished to avoid; and all have been anxious for the attentions of someone whom they wished to please. (*Chapter 10*)

Now, at last, we are fully engaged with the author and her characters in sympathising with 'the common feelings of common life.' Catherine narrowly misses having to dance with John Thorpe who has casually assumed that she will be his partner. His disappointment at losing Catherine, however loudly expressed, is short-lived. Free of John Thorpe's coarseness, Catherine finds herself drawn into a conversation with Henry which is at a quite different level from anything we have so far been offered in the novel. His comparison of matrimony and dancing is thoughtful, intelligent and extended. Although it is conducted with an apparently impersonal politeness, it is not irrelevant to their situation. He clearly wants to know how free Catherine is from involvement with John Thorpe, and he is finally rewarded by Catherine's naive avowal of interest in himself.

Catherine is no jaded sophisticate; she is honest, simple and enthusiastic, and these qualities are enough to endear her to Henry. Jane Austen hurries forward the progress of the novel by having her heroine noticed by Henry's father, and by engaging Catherine to take a walk with Henry and his sister the next day. Catherine's last word to them is an appeal to their fidelity to keep the appointment: it is, of course, just the subject of faithfulness which has been the topic of Catherine's conversation with Henry. The episode which follows is a test of Catherine's good faith.

Catherine's dilemma arises from the fact that she had promised to go for a walk in the country unless it rained. In fact, it does rain, and the Tilneys do not arrive. Unfortunately, the Thorpes and her brother do, begging her to come for a long drive. Should she go? To help her to decide, John Thorpe says they will visit a castle, which Catherine thinks will be like one of the castles in the romantic novels she has been reading. He also says that he has seen Henry Tilney driving off with a pretty girl. Mrs Allen, appealed to for advice, merely bows to the pressure of the majority. Just as she is driving away from Bath, meditating 'by turns, on broken promises and broken arches, phaetons and false hangings, Tilneys and trap-doors' (Chapter 11), she sees the Tilneys looking back at her. Catherine finds that John Thorpe has lied to her about seeing Henry Tilney. When put to the test, his horse cannot get as far as he had hoped. After seven miles they judge it prudent to turn back. Of course, Catherine is not to blame for what has happened, but she has made an error of judgment in believing John Thorpe, whose idle boasting has been exposed by a practical test, and she has failed to be guided by her own sense of what she ought to do: it is a minor, but palpable, breach of her word, which Catherine finds painful.

The Tilneys have called, but no message has been left. She is further mortified when Mr Allen says that their excursion was 'a strange, wild scheme'
(Chapter 11). It is Catherine's first lesson in the value of acting on principle.
Making her apologies to the Tilneys turns out to be less straightforward
than she supposes. Catherine is hurt by their refusal to admit her: it appears
a deliberate snub. At the theatre, Henry Tilney's recognition of her seems
perfunctory. There is a hint of mystery about how she has been treated,
though Catherine believes she has been guilty of some unforgivable social
offence. Once again it is Catherine's directness which melts Henry
Tilney's reserve. Accused of being offended with her, he replies:

> 'Me! — I take offence!'
> 'Nay, I am sure by your look, when you came into the box, you were
> angry.'
> 'I angry! I could have no right!'
> 'Well, nobody would have thought you had no right who saw your
> face.' (*Chapter 12*)

Henry's words imply that their relationship is not deep enough for either to
have a claim upon the other; Catherine's naive response, however, suggests that the feelings people have for one another create attachments and
mutual obligations. His right to be angry with her springs from the sense
that she has betrayed him.

Now Jane Austen repeats the little motif which led to Catherine's first moral
dilemma: the plan to visit Bristol is resumed, just when she has renewed her
promise to walk in the country with the Tilneys. It is a common enough
dilemma; how is to be resolved? James Morland says she must go with them, as
if the mere fact of numbers settled the matter. She feels the strength of their
hostility and is hurt enough by Isabella's unkindness to drop her arm. Once
more John Thorpe tries to force her to do what he wants — this time by telling
Miss Tilney the story of a previous engagement which they have concocted.
Now Catherine is physically beset by them as they try to force her not to go to
Miss Tilney in person, but she insists: 'if I could not be persuaded into doing
what I thought wrong, I will never be tricked into it!' (Chapter 13).

On this occasion Catherine is able to make the grounds of her behaviour
explicit to herself:

> Setting her own inclination apart, to have failed a second time in her
> engagement to Miss Tilney, to have retracted a promise voluntarily
> made only five minutes before, and on a false pretence too, must have
> been wrong. She had not been withstanding them on selfish principles
> alone, she had not consulted merely her own gratification . . . no, she
> had attended to what was due to others, and to her own character in their
> opinion. (*Chapter 13*)

However duty may be related to feelings, her sense of what she ought to do does not simply depend on what she wants. Her previous behaviour has created a web of obligations and expectations which cannot be cut short at the behest of a privileged group of friends. Catherine's sense of her own integrity partly depends on how she is seen by others. To damage her reputation in their eyes is to damage herself.

It would be a mistake to think these debates are about trifles. Catherine is gradually becoming an autonomous individual who understands, as Mrs Allen does not, what a moral question is. Mrs Allen believes that one should do as others do and that appearance is everything, but she has no means of knowing how conflicts should be resolved. When Catherine returns from her visit of explanation to the Tilneys, where she has been graciously received by Henry's father, the General, she asks Mr Allen whether she was right not to break the engagement with the Tilneys. Mr Allen not only agrees that she was right but expresses his disapproval of young men and women 'driving about the country in open carriages.' Pressed on the point, Mrs Allen agrees with him, because clean gowns are apt to be splashed in open carriges. Whatever our opinion may be about the propriety of young men and women 'going to inns and public places together', it seems clear that the point cannot be settled by reference to whether their clothes are likely to get dirty. Mrs Allen defends herself by telling Catherine that young people like to have their own way. But Catherine's reply is surely the reply of young people of all generations to their negligent elders: 'But this was something of real consequence; and I do not think you would have found me hard to persuade' (Chapter 13). There *are* moral problems; occasionally, it is helpful to discuss them with an older friend: but Mrs Allen has eyes for nothing but her muslins.

In the episode that follows—the walk to Beechen Cliff (Chapter 14)— Catherine is to learn that appearances are deceptive, while Jane Austen herself reveals her complexity of vision and wit. In the company of the Tilneys, Catherine finds herself out of her depth. Luckily, she has Eleanor Tilney to mediate between her and Henry's exuberant self-assurance. Jane Austen's jokes here are double-edged: some are against Catherine's ignorant enthusiasm; some are against Henry's school-masterly preciseness. Eleanor Tilney displays a warm-hearted intelligence which suggests that it is possible to be clever and considerate for the feelings of others. Henry Tilney is presented as a man who does not disdain to enjoy civilised pleasures merely because women enjoy them too: like Catherine, he enjoys reading novels. But when he takes Catherine to task for her inexact use of the word 'nice', Eleanor Tilney comes to her rescue. He is 'more nice than wise'; in pursuing a pedantic exactness, he is in danger of being more concerned with words than with things—in this case, with the feelings of Catherine. More gently, she explores her interests, and provides a reason for enjoying history, even if some of it is merely the invention of historians. Jane Austen's purpose seems to be the dissolution of sexual stereotypes: if a man can enjoy reading novels, why should a young woman not enjoy reading which demands 'very severe, very intense application.' Need instruction be equated with torture? Even if Henry Tilney is pedantic, Catherine's interest in reading seems very narrowly based. When the Tilneys turn to discuss the aesthetics of landscapes, she is lost, though Jane Austen mischievously suggests that Catherine's ignorance may not deter a lover who is anxious to display his knowledge.

Throughout this scene, Jane Austen's irony is high-spirited and comprehensive: it is sad to be narrowly educated, but clever people can be silly; it is wrong to make too much fuss over words, but foolish to misuse them so that people are misled about things. Elaborate theories about art and aesthetics have their place but they are useless if they stop us enjoying the view. Running beneath the banter of the chapter is a serious question about the intellectual capacity of women. Are they inferior to men in understanding? Eleanor Tilney defends her brother by saying that 'he must be entirely misunderstood, if he can appear to say an unjust thing of any woman at all, or an unkind one of me.' Catherine is very ready to believe her, but Henry's expressed commendation of women has been ambiguous. If it is true that, as he says, 'Nature has given them so much, that they never find it necessary to use more than half', they may fairly be accused of a failure to use their powers to the full.

For a moment, it is as if Jane Austen's narrator has lost faith in her heroine as she descends from 'the excess of her pleasure' at being with the Tilneys to the mere amiability of being back with Mrs Allen. There is a further descent when Catherine is re-united with her friends, finds she has to listen to a recital of female jealousies and is astonished to learn that Isabella not only loves her brother but is engaged to him.

The narrator's description of Catherine's reception of this news is not sympathetic:

> Never had Catherine listened to any thing so full of interest, wonder and joy. Her brother and her friend engaged! — New to such circumstances, the importance of it appeared unspeakably great, and she contemplated it as one of those grand events, of which the ordinary course of life can hardly afford a return. The strength of her feelings she could not express; the nature of them, however, contented her friend. The happiness of having such a sister was their first effusion, and the fair ladies mingled in embraces and tears of joy. (*Chapter 15*)

The rhythm of that final sentence, and its diction — 'their first effusion', 'the fair ladies', 'mingled', 'embraces and tears of joy' — make it clear that Catherine is for the moment no longer 'my heroine', but merely a 'heroine of fiction' — the simpering, extravagant woman exemplified in this novel only by Isabella Thorpe. Isabella Thorpe, one might say, has momentarily transformed Jane Austen's heroine into the likeness of herself. How can she escape? The answer is that Catherine is too sensible to share Isabella's mood or language for long. Isabella's assertion that she will be 'so much more attached to my dear Morland's family than to my own' is 'a pitch of friendship beyond Catherine', who finds it equally impossible to share in Isabella's exaggerated admiration for her brother. Although Isabella reminds her of the behaviour of the heroines of fiction, common sense keeps suggesting that her behaviour is unreal. For the reader Isabella's language is an extended exercise in the absurd:

> Where people are really attached, poverty itself is wealth: grandeur I detest: I could not settle in London for the universe. A cottage in some retired village would be extasy. There are some charming little villas about Richmond. (*Chapter 15*)

This is the language of the theatre: its paradoxes ('poverty is wealth') bear no examination, since we know that Isabella's ways of speaking are not directly related to her intentions: her wish to appear simple is immediately contradicted by her real desire for wealth.

Mr and Mrs Morland are perfectly willing to consent to their son's marriage and to promise to help him; Mr and Mrs Allen seem undisturbed by the news. Catherine is too eager to go to dinner with the Tilneys to notice John Thorpe's clumsy attempts to propose to her. But he thinks she has given him every encouragement to try again. Her encounter with John Thorpe is enough to restore Catherine to polite self-possession and good sense.

## Volume 2 (*Chapters 16–31*)

Catherine's visit to the Tilneys in Milsom Street begins a movement that takes her away from the Thorpes into the unfamiliar social world of Northanger Abbey. Despite Catherine's anticipations, it has not been a success. She cannot account for the restraint under which she found the family, though she does not credit Isabella's accusations that the family is proud and Henry Tilney inconstant. In the absence of James Morland, Isabella pretends not to want to attend the evening's ball, at which she expects to meet Henry's elder soldier brother. The expectations of the habitual novel-reader — that Captain Tilney is planning to kidnap Catherine — are matched in fatuity by Catherine's perfectly human suspicion that he is liable to set his brother against her, by repeating some unfounded gossip. The unbridled fantasy of fiction-writers, Jane Austen implies, is an organised version of the floating fantasy generated spontaneously by human insecurity.

Isabella's unaccountable decision to dance with Captain Tilney, who has declared himself indifferent to dancing, provides Henry and Catherine with another subject for conversation. Catherine's belief that Isabella is moved to do so only by good-nature seems to him to prove her own lack of guile. Once again, it is Catherine's simplicity which Henry finds attractive, a simplicity which her character abounds in when it is free from the artificial language and ideas of Isabella, whose catalogue of excuses for dancing with Captain Tilney ends with the confession that she did it because he was handsome and everyone was watching them. The full extent of the hard calculation under her romantic veneer is revealed when she learns what the income of her future husband is likely to be. Her protestations of unselfishness do not mask her interest in money and her willingness to blame those who appear to deny her it. Sensing that her true motives are suspected, she hurriedly shifts her ground: it is the delay that Mr Morland's arrangements impose on the marriage — not the arrangements themselves — that distress her.

Catherine has just learned that the Tilneys are to leave Bath: her disappointment turns to joy when the General invites her to stay (Chapter 17). But there is a puzzle about the manner of the invitation: Eleanor Tilney makes it with some embarrassment; the General's reinforcement of it is exceedingly fulsome, and it appears he has previously asked the Allens if she may come. Catherine is overjoyed; the very name of the Tilneys' home enchants her. She is bathed in a flood of self-congratulation: 'Everything seemed to co-operate for her advantage.' But the narration maintains an ironic note, as it reports: 'Her passion for ancient edifices was next in degree to her passion for Henry Tilney', and 'with all the chances against her of house, hall, place, park, court, and cottage, Northanger turned up an abbey, and she was to be its inhabitant.' The ironic note is unmistakable: what is its justification? The general answer seems to be that the narrator — and, therefore, the author — has an ambiguous view of Catherine's simplicity. Admirable in some respects, in others it is insufficient. Love for ancient buildings is not the same as love for people: the two 'passions' cannot be equated.

One of the defects of Catherine's simplicity is her blindness about Isabella. The narrative itself has taught the reader that Isabella's words are no clue to her thoughts and are usually at variance with her actions. Catherine learns these facts more slowly. Thus, Isabella on a morning visit to the Pump Room returns to a corner of the room which gives her a full view of its entrances. Who is she looking for? — no one. Her thoughts are never where her eyes are directed. Who is she thinking of? The answer comes in her next sentence, when she refers — by his surname — to Captain Tilney, a mode of address which she has hitherto reserved for her fiancé, James Morland. When, attracted by Isabella's stare, Captain Tilney approaches them, Catherine begins to suspect there may be something between them. She is sufficiently angry with Isabella to leave her with Captain Tilney, but she still does not believe she is treacherous. Jane Austen has planted clues to alert the reader to Isabella's possible change of mind: her reference to 'Tilney', her talk of 'harmless flirtations' and youthful changes of mind are clear indications of her thinking.

When Catherine discusses Isabella's conduct with Henry Tilney, the tone of the narrative is graver and more penetrating. Even if she does not know it—and Catherine assumes she does not—Isabella's toleration of Frederick Tilney's attentions must cause James Morland pain. Catherine assumes that Captain Tilney does not know of her engagement, but Henry assures her that he does. James Morland's anguish is Isabella's responsibility. But Henry is reassuring: Isabella and James must know their own minds best. It would be no compliment to either to suggest that Isabella will be safe only if Captain Tilney is absent. Besides, it will all blow over when the Captain returns to his regiment. Catherine is reassured:

> [She] would contend no longer against comfort. She had resisted its approaches during the whole length of a speech, but it now carried her captive. Henry Tilney must know best. She blamed herself for the extent of her fears, and resolved never to think so seriously on the subject again. (*Chapter 19*)

Here is a woman writing with penetrating candour about the psychological processes of her sisters. The strong temptation for women like Catherine to believe that men know best lies in the freedom from mental effort which the belief confers: it had been easy for Catherine to see that breaking promises is wrong, even if the social pressure to do so was strong. It is not so easy for her to see that she cannot evade the duty of serious thinking. But Jane Austen's metaphor is revealing: 'comfort', which seems so appealing, is an enemy of freedom; a responsible attention to the value of one's personal impressions is a condition of moral health.

The transition to Northanger Abbey (Chapter 20) is accompanied by further examples of the General's uncertain temper: he is querulous, exacting yet strangely attentive to Catherine. He encourages her to drive with Henry in his curricle, and she is torn between delight and distress at being alone with him. When Henry asks if she is 'prepared to encounter all the horrors that a building such as "what one reads about" may produce?', he begins to construct a Gothic Tale in which she takes the leading part. In his account all the unlikely events of the novels she has recently read are summarised. Their essential ingredients bear some relationship to characteristics which Jane Austen has analysed in the behaviour of her own characters. On the one hand, Henry's tale abounds in contradictions, not unlike those displayed by Isabella: unconquerable feelings are conquered; impenetrable mysteries are instantly laid bare. On the other hand, the heroine of the tale is carried along by irresistible forces, which determine her behaviour. Jane Austen's parody is not simply literary; she is attempting to destroy by ridicule an alternative, and threatening account, of how human beings should behave and what their lives are like.

Although Northanger Abbey turns out to be a comfortable modern house, Catherine is now too saturated with expectations of romantic horror not to want to be astonished. The real danger in Northanger Abbey is the General's obsessive concern for punctuality. A hint of the reason for the General's interest in Catherine is given by his assumption that Mr Allen's house is grander than his own. But Catherine's attention is absorbed by the possibility of romantic adventure in the darkened Abbey, swept now by a storm. Although her fantasies about 'a large high chest' have already received an embarrassing check, she begins to weave a web of possibilities around a lacquer cabinet in her bedroom. Opinions may differ about the effectiveness of the passages that follow. Coming after Henry's parody of the Gothic novel, they may appear laboured. The humour lies in Catherine's credulous acceptance that what Henry told her might be true. Now we have left the world of literary parody; Jane Austen is exploring an ordinary girl's capacity for fantasy. Catherine's behaviour now is much below her best: having inadvertently extinguished her candle, she stands 'motionless with horror':

> Darkness impenetrable and immoveable filled the room. A violent gust of wind, rising with sudden fury, added fresh horror to the moment. Catherine trembled from head to foot. In the pause which succeeded, a sound like receding footsteps and the closing of a distant door struck on her affrighted ear. Human nature could support no more. (*Chapter 21*)

The bathos is deliberate: Catherine is suffering from an overheated imagination which any physical sensation will feed with morbid fear. This is not parody: it is an attempt to convey the impressions of self-induced hysteria. Is it consistent with what we know of Catherine? Only if we accept that Jane Austen is attempting to portray the ambiguous nature of simplicity. Catherine is guileless enough to be unsuspicious of Isabella, credulous enough to be wary of 'an immense heavy chest' and 'an old-fashioned black cabinet'. Failing to notice objective fact, the human mind can furnish its surroundings with unreal substance of its own devising. The character of Catherine Morland is a study of immaturity, which is dependent for its strength on familiar surroundings. Overtaken by sleep, she awakens next day to a common-sense perception of the unthreatening objects of every – day life, her 'precious manuscript' a laundry-list and farrier's bill. When the fantasies of the darkness are dispelled by clear morning light, Catherine is ashamed:

> Nothing could now be clearer than the absurdity of her recent fancies. To suppose that a manuscript of many generations back could have remained undiscovered in a room such as that, so modern, so habitable! — or that she should be the first to possess the skill of unlocking a cabinet, the key of which was open to all!
> How could she have so imposed on herself? (*Chapter 22*)

There is nothing subtle or oblique about this piece of self-deception. There is a danger that in taking the substance of the Gothic novel seriously, Catherine is simply in danger of looking foolish to the reader as much as to herself. Having made herself feel foolish, Catherine is anxious that Henry should not know of it, but once again her fancy runs away with her, weaving unflattering stories round the General and his dead wife. The real purpose of her visit is now clear to everyone but Catherine. For reasons of his own the General has decided that she will be a suitable wife for Henry: his generous treatment of her, his willingness to show her round his home, clearly testify to his sense of her worth. Oblivious to all this, Catherine continues to fantasise about the cause of the General's wife's death; indeed, she begins to think she may not be dead at all, but still maintained alive somewhere within the rooms of the Abbey the General has not shown her. The exposure of this further fantasy is protracted: Jane Austen uses the General's uncertain temper to lend some credibility to Catherine's sense that there is some mystery about his relationships with his family. Having failed to visit the room of the late Mrs Tilney in the company of her daughter, Catherine decides to go by herself. The room is bright, well-furnished and carefully maintained; it is, of course, empty. When Henry surprises her by arriving by a back staircase, she is too alarmed not to conceal what has been in her mind. His quick grasp of her suspicions, his explanation of how his mother died, and his reproof of her idle surmises perhaps come ill from the man who has first stirred her romantic fancies about the Abbey. But they are a classic rebuttal of the conventions of Gothic romance:

> 'Dear Miss Morland, consider the dreadful nature of the suspicions you have entertained. What have you been judging from? Remember the country and the age in which we live. Remember that we are English, that we are Christians. Consult your own understanding, your own sense of the probable, your own observation of what is passing around you— Does our education prepare us for such atrocities? Do our laws connive at them?' (*Chapter 24*)

While the first incidence of Catherine's fantasies may be defended on psychological grounds, it is less obvious that the second can be. Henry's rebuke is delivered more to the writers of the 'thrillers' of the time than to the young woman whose faltering steps to maturity we have been following in this novel. Here he is more a mouthpiece of his creator's literary judgment than a young man speaking to the girl he loves. Perhaps it may be thought that this episode shows Catherine in too bad a light: she is fantasising about a much-loved mother and seriously exposing herself to a charge of bad taste as well as stupidity. Can her reputation really survive such levity of character?

We can forgive Catherine only because she is totally contrite and miraculously restored to good sense. What she has been guilty of is the wilful satisfaction of a perverse desire for terror. Although the source of the stimulation is firmly located in her course of reading with Isabella at Bath, there is no mention of Henry's part in recalling this material to her mind and providing the immediate source of her fantasies. What follows is Jane Austen's literary manifesto, a statement of what she regarded as the aims of fiction:

> Charming as were all Mrs Radcliffe's works, and charming even as were the works of all her imitators, it was not in them perhaps that human nature, at least in the midland counties of England, was to be looked for. Of the Alps and the Pyrenees, with their pine forests and their vices, they might give a faithful delineation . . . But in the central part of England there was surely some security for the existence even of a wife not beloved, in the laws of the land, and the manners of the age. (*Chapter 25*)

It may be felt that Jane Austen is using her heroine to change the perceptions of the reading public and to establish new criteria for the writing of fiction; but the literary purposes of the author have strayed from the psychological and moral problems of her heroine.

The final section of the novel opens Catherine's eyes to the character of the General. Although his behaviour to his own children has been exacting and peremptory, and although it is clear that he inspires them with something more than respect, his treatment of Catherine has been unfailingly deferential. His departure to London lightens the atmosphere at Northanger Abbey. Despite her doubts about Henry's feelings for her, Catherine is pressed to stay longer by Eleanor and she has no doubt about the goodwill of the General. The reversal of her good fortune, brought about by the General's sudden return and his decision that she should leave the house the next day, is carefully prepared for. Henry's duties take him to Woodston; the young women are left on their own; Catherine hears the unexpected arrival of a carriage, and expects a difficult meeting with Captain Tilney for whom she knows Isabella has recently rejected her brother. The agitated noises outside her door resemble those which inspired her night fears, but this time Catherine is in control of her feelings and the troubles are real ones. Now Catherine feels the weight of the General's decisiveness: she is to leave at seven o'clock the next morning and is to travel on her own. Eleanor's embarrassment at conveying the message is increased by her powerlessness to alter its terms. She is all too aware of the affront it offers to Catherine and to her family and friends. Now she has a real cause for sleeplessness and Jane Austen does not fail to draw a parallel with her previous night of distress:

> That room, in which her disturbed imagination had tormented her on her first arrival, was again the scene of agitated spirits and unquiet slumbers. Yet how different now the source of her inquietude from what it had been then—how mournfully superior in reality and substance! (*Chapter 28*)

In her account of Catherine's journey home Jane Austen contrasts her anxious speculations about her dismisal, and Henry's reaction to it, with the concerned, but sustaining, reflections of her parents on what has taken place. Catherine's own thoughts are sad enough, but now they are rooted in memory and absorbed in the contemplation of possibilities. But these preoccupations are selfish, obsessive and fruitless. Once home, she is restored to the affection and sympathy of her family, and reminded of the limits there are to the understanding of human behaviour. Mrs Morland's sensible view is that Catherine will have gained in maturity and self-possession from her puzzling experiences. But her family's consolation has not done justice to the force of Catherine's awakened consciousness. Her acquaintance with the Tilneys—and with Henry in particular—has made it impossible for her to be content in future with the banality of life at Fullerton.

What follows is a characteristic unravelling of what passes for mystery in *Northanger Abbey*: the explanation takes us back to Chapter 12 when John Thorpe was seen talking to General Tilney. It is perfectly in character that he should have given the General a false impression of Catherine's financial position: he had represented her father as being respectably well-off and had said she was likely to inherit Mr Allen's estate. In return for this information, the General had no compunction in making it his business to blight the hopes of John Thorpe and to promote the interests of Henry, giving his son 'an almost positive command . . . of doing everything in his power to attach [Catherine]' (Chapter 30). No matter what power General Tilney has over his family, it is difficult to reconcile the self-possessed young man we meet in the novel with such an abject role. John Thorpe has not been slow to contradict himself, and the General has no doubt formed his own conclusions about Catherine's prospects of wealth from Mr Allen. Jane Austen is boldly perfunctory in her account of those matters, offering a brisk summary, and leaving the reader to imagine how the details might have come out. Catherine's dismissal has roused Henry to the disobedience of travelling immediately to Fullerton to propose. Now, author and reader are both aware that not much more of the story is left to be told. *Northanger Abbey* is after all 'only a novel'; the final task of the novelist is to produce a tidy conclusion. Mr and Mrs Morland have rejoiced in the prospect of having Henry as a son-in-law. They have only stipulated that his father should consent to his marriage. Eleanor's marriage to a wealthy man softens his heart. Mr Morland turns out to be wealthier than the General had feared and Catherine's prospects as heiress to Fullerton not so uncertain as had been reported. The author ends her novel in the sardonic vein of the juvenilia, putting her characters back in the box as if they had been puppets all the time and making fun of her own performance.

The ending of the novel is worthy of the clever facetiousness of the young Jane Austen, but it is not perhaps a quite fitting conclusion to a novel which, however lacking in integration, however marred by genuine failures of serious purpose, does stand as a kind of artistic manifesto. Underneath the youthful high spirits, the delight in parody, the verbal acrobatics and constructional play, there lies the affirmation that the novel is more than a game, that it can offer some reflective critique of current modes of life. Jane Austen has learnt that she can do more than make fun of existing kinds of novel; a new and honourable kind of art-form lies waiting to be discovered.

Chapter 3

# *Sense and Sensibility*:
## the consolations
## of self-control

## Introduction

According to a memorandum by Cassandra Austen, *Sense and Sensibility* was begun in November 1797 when Jane Austen was twenty-two, immediately after the completion of *First Impressions*, which was the original of *Pride and Prejudice*. But Cassandra also says that some version of the story had been written earlier and called *Elinor and Marianne*: it has been suggested that this earlier version took the form of a series of letters. *Sense and Sensibility* was first published in 1811, after it had undergone considerable revision, although it is not possible to form any idea as to what these revisions were or when they were undertaken. On the evidence of the novel as it stands, *Sense and Sensibility* represents an early stage of Jane Austen's art as a novelist, but perhaps it can be said that she is now writing with a full commitment to the seriousness of her art. As originally published, it consisted of three volumes: Volume One contained Chapters 1–22; Volume Two, Chapters 23–36; Volume Three, Chapters 37–50.

## Commentary

**Volume One (*Chapters 1–22*)**

Mrs Henry Dashwood is a widow with three daughters — Elinor, Marianne and Margaret — who has been left badly off by the death of her husband. Her step-son, Mr John Dashwood, and his wife, Fanny, having earnestly reconsidered John's promise to help them, decide from the best of motives to do as little as possible. Mrs Dashwood accepts the offer of a cottage near a large estate in Devon called Barton Park which has been made by a distant relative, Sir John Middleton. Before they leave, Elinor is attracted to Fanny Dashwood's brother, Edward Ferrars. She hopes he will visit them in Devon, but it is clear that neither Fanny nor her mother thinks Elinor good enough for Edward. At Barton Park they meet Sir John Middleton, a sociable, rather officious man, his well-bred but rather cold-hearted wife and her cheerful, talkative, rather vulgar mother, Mrs Jennings. Another visitor is Colonel Brandon, a grave, reserved man of thirty-five, who shows an interest in Marianne, although, for her part, she considers him to be quite elderly.

Elinor and Marianne are both lively and intelligent girls but Marianne prizes enthusiasm and feeling above any other quality, while Elinor prefers good sense. One day Marianne is rescued from a nasty fall by a handsome young man called Willoughby. Soon she is in love with him, and Colonel Brandon appears to have no chance against such youthful ardour. Everyone begins to assume that Marianne and Willoughby are engaged. But then two surprising events occur: first, Colonel Brandon is obliged to leave for London, then Willoughby announces that he must go there too—he does not know when he will return. Marianne is overwhelmed with grief. Unexpectedly, Edward Ferrars arrives, but he appears cold and out of spirits. Elinor blames his mother for his strange behaviour, but, when he leaves too, unlike Marianne, she maintains her composure.

At this point Mr and Mrs Palmer, daughter and son-in-law of Mrs Jennings arrive at Barton Park. She is pleasant and cheerful; her husband is morose and rather rude. Mrs Palmer, who turns out to be a neighbour of Willoughby's, has heard that Marianne is engaged to him. She hopes the Dashwood girls will visit her in London during the winter. After the departure of the Palmers, Miss Anne and Miss Lucy Steele, cousins of Mrs Jennings, are introduced. The Steeles are rather disagreeably ingratiating. Elinor is surprised to find that they know Edward Ferrars and horrified when Lucy Steele tells her that she is engaged to him.

Let us now consider in detail how Jane Austen shapes her material. The death of Mr Dashwood subverts the security of the Dashwood family. But it also reveals hidden instability: there is a tension between the women who remain and the heir to the estate, Mr John Dashwood. He has made his father a promise to look after his sisters, and his failure to fulfil this promise provides a continuing subsidiary source of the action of the novel. Jane Austen establishes the mean-spiritedness of Mr and Mrs John Dashwood as a sour joke to which she can return. If the Dashwood family is an imperfect mixture of selfishness (in John Dashwood), fortitude (in Elinor) and emotional excess (in Marianne and her mother), this flawed human pattern is extended as we meet the Ferrars family and the Middletons, through whom we are led to the Palmers and the Steeles. Willoughby, the outsider who meets the Dashwoods by chance, is himself a character of contradictions, a mixture of generosity and selfishness, of enthusiasm and calculation. Through the girl he has seduced, he is linked with Colonel Brandon, a man of complete integrity of character. It is easy to see how the pattern of stability and change, which forms the matrix for the novel, is repeated in the fabric of the human material from which the action flows. Jane Austen values, and wishes to recommend, the integrity of character displayed by

Elinor and Edward and Colonel Brandon, but it is only by contrast with the instability of Marianne or the faithlessness of Willoughby that their virtue can be understood.

Having established the initial situation and introduced her characters, Jane Austen develops her story by methods of surprise and discovery. The first mystery is Colonel Brandon's departure for London on the very morning of an expedition which he has arranged for the party at Barton Park. His departure is followed by the equally abrupt disappearance of Willoughby. Bereft of the men whose presence has enlivened the company, Elinor and Marianne are left to think about their own attitudes and feelings. The differences between them become more apparent: Elinor's feelings are private and under the control of her reason. She considers the puzzles and mysteries of life rationally and objectively. Marianne prizes feeling as a form of knowledge; she believes it can be treated as a dependable source of immediate understanding. Jane Austen uses the events of the novel as a means of testing these attitudes and beliefs.

Now, she re-introduces Edward Ferrars, whose behaviour raises new questions. At Norland his friendship with Elinor had been obvious. Why has he taken so long to visit them at Barton? Who has he been visiting at Plymouth? Whose hair is in the ring he wears on his finger? Why is he so melancholy? Why does he go away again so soon? These questions are left unanswered, as first the Palmers, then the Steeles are introduced. The Palmers widen the social circle but do not advance the action to any great extent, although they do extend the setting of the novel from the country to London, and as neighbours of Willoughby are attached to another strand of the plot. Their main function is to offer another picture of marriage, that haven towards which the unmarried young women of the novel are directed. They are a union of opposites—he is intelligent and rude; she is warm-hearted and silly. They move through life in a state of mutual incomprehension. As exemplified by the Palmers, marriage is a state of frustration and discord.

The Steeles play a far more significant part: the elder Miss Steele is a spinster whose constant references to an admirer are an obvious fantasy, and whose indiscretions require to be managed by her more tactful sister. As might be expected in an English novel, it is their speech which betrays the fact that they are not quite ladies. Lucy Steele soon tells Elinor about her secret engagement to Edward Ferrars, a confidence which throws light on the last of the puzzles left unresolved in the first volume of the novel—namely, his strange behaviour on his visit to Barton. Elinor's response to the news is, of course, of crucial significance. She mentally tests what Lucy has told her against the information she already has. It is the case that the picture Lucy shows her is of Edward Ferrars. She has no reason to doubt what Lucy has told her; Lucy appears to have heard of her discretion and good sense from Edward and, as a consequence, is willing to trust

Elinor with her secret. Lucy says he had been with her uncle, his former tutor, before he visited the Dashwoods at Barton—which is consonant with Edward's account of his visit to friends near Plymouth. Lucy says that when he left them he was out of spirits. The lock of hair set in a ring was Lucy's own, she says. The questions posed in Chapter 19 receive specific answers in Chapter 22. When Elinor is convinced by Lucy's story:

> . . . for a few moments, she was almost overcome—her heart sunk within her, and she could hardly stand; but exertion was indispensably necessary, and she struggled so resolutely against the oppression of her feelings that her success was speedy, and for the time complete. (*Chapter 22*)

When Lucy asks Elinor if she saw the ring on Edward's finger—the ring which (in Chapter 18) he had said was his sister's and which Elinor had thought was her own:

> 'I did,' said Elinor with a composure of voice, under which was concealed an emotion and distress beyond any thing she had ever felt before. She was mortified, shocked, confounded. (*Chapter 22*)

But the conversation soon comes to an end, 'and Elinor was then at liberty to think and be wretched'. There is no question about the strength of Elinor's feelings. But she refuses to be overwhelmed by them. She believes in independence, so far as that is possible to someone still financially dependent, and dependent on others for a tolerable social life. She will not hurt other people by unloading her feelings on them. Her aim is 'self-command'; her means of attaining it 'exertion'.

---

## Volume Two (*Chapters 23–36*)

---

Elinor still believes in Edward's affection for her; she can only suppose that his engagement to Lucy Steele is the mistake of an immature young man. She says nothing about what Lucy has told her. In January Mrs Jennings invites the girls to go with her to London where Marianne hopes to meet Willoughby, but he fails to appear. When they meet him by chance at a party, he seems embarrassed and greets Marianne coldly. A letter from him the next day breaks off the relationship. It appears that he is to marry a rich young woman. Marianne is greatly distressed. It is at this point that Colonel Brandon reveals that Willoughby has seduced and deserted his (Colonel Brandon's) ward, and that it was on this girl's behalf that Colonel Brandon had been urgently summoned to London. Willoughby's behaviour appears thoroughly unprincipled. John Dashwood and his wife arrive in London with the news that Edward Ferrars is to marry a rich woman. Edward's family is unaware of his secret engagement to Lucy Steele. Indeed, Lucy's willingness to please endears her to Fanny Dashwood and

Lady Middleton, whose cold sense of social correctness has soon made them friends. Lucy Steele is convinced that Fanny and Mrs Ferrars have taken a liking to her; she does not realise that she is only preferred to Elinor Dashwood because she is regarded as less of a threat to Edward's prospects of marrying well. Although John Dashwood believes that it is his duty to invite his sisters to stay with him in London, Fanny prefers to invite Anne and Lucy Steele.

The second volume of the novel contrasts Elinor's attitudes with Marianne's response to the gradual unravelling of the mystery about Willoughby. But first, in Chapter 24, Jane Austen uses a conversation between Lucy and Elinor to redress the balance of advantage between them. Elinor does not feel that she can tell the news to anyone else, and it is an embarrassment to her that the match-makers at Barton have linked Edward's name to hers. She is convinced that Edward has made a youthful mistake, but she cannot accuse him of behaving badly to her. Even if Edward's first attachment to Lucy was a blunder, Elinor accepts that the promise he has made cannot be withdrawn. Now, as she talks to Lucy, she is able to examine the kind of relationship Edward and Lucy have. Although Lucy has not lied to her about the engagement, she is less trustworthy when she speaks about her feelings. She is a little too certain of what Edward feels about her; she is too anxious to assert that she has no cause for alarm, no suspicion of any rival. Her worries about Edward's prospects, and her mistrust of his mother's intentions, allow Jane Austen to offer a hint about how their engagement will run. For the first time there is mention of Mr Robert Ferrars.

In retrospect, the student of the novel can see that Jane Austen has carefully planted suggestions which will have an effect later in the story. These hints are a preliminary sketch for events which do not take shape until the public anouncement of Lucy's engagement in Volume Three, when the reaction of Edward's mother to Lucy is quite different from Lucy's present expectations. Now we return to the testing of Marianne. The succession of disappointments which leads to the news that Willoughby has deserted her to marry a rich woman occupies most of the central section of the novel. It is a tale of 'guilt and misery', of the kind which in *Mansfield Park* Jane Austen declares she will leave to other pens. Marianne's despairing impatience to see Willoughby, his strange failure to write to her, his refusal to go to Lady Middleton's ball, his distant behaviour to her when they do at last meet, and the cruelty of his final letter to her are all recorded in painful detail. In comparing her own situation with Marianne's, Elinor can only feel sadness and concern for her sister:

> . . . while she could *esteem* Edward as much as ever, however they might be divided in future, her mind might always be supported. But every circumstance that could embitter such an evil seemed uniting to heighten the misery of Marianne in a final separation from Willoughby . . . *(Chapter 28)*

While unhappiness may be unavoidable in human life, Jane Austen firmly makes the point that a scrupulous adherence to right action—which must imply consideration for others—will eliminate the kind of misery Marianne is suffering from. There is no attempt to soften the intensity of Marianne's feelings and no suggestions that they are spurious. When Willoughby's final letter comes,

> Elinor . . . eager at all events to know what Willoughby had written, hurried away to their room, where, on opening the door, she saw Marianne stretched on the bed, almost choked with grief. . . . Elinor drew near . . . and seating herself on the bed, took her hand, kissed her affectionately several times, and then gave way to a burst of tears, which at first was scarcely less violent than Marianne's. The latter, though unable to speak, seemed to feel all the tenderness of this behaviour . . . and then covering her face with her handkerchief, almost screamed with agony. (*Chapter 29*)

It is not the kind of scene that readers with a conventional idea of Jane Austen's work might expect to find. It is raw and indecorous. At this crisis both Elinor and Marianne give way to bitter and vehement grief. *Sense and Sensibility* dwells much on 'misery'—the word is constantly repeated—not all of it imaginary or exaggerated. The betrayal of human affection causes pain, and Jane Austen records the fact accurately. But we cannot believe that her sympathy is still with Marianne when she says:

> ' . . . misery such as mine has no pride. I care not who knows that I am wretched. The triumph of seeing me so may be open to all the world. Elinor, Elinor, they who suffer so little may be proud and independent as they like—may resist insult, or return mortification—but I cannot. I must feel—I must be wretched—and they are welcome to enjoy the consciousness of it that can.' (*Chapter 29*)

Such unashamed self-expression is unlikely to gain the sympathy of Jane Austen, though it has the ring of the later Victorian heroines of Charlotte Brontë.

Once again, however, a narrative thread has been thrown out which Jane Austen will develop later. In the depths of her misery and the wildness of her grief, Marianne insists on having the comfort of believing that it is not Willoughby who has betrayed her. She has no evidence for this belief—unlike Elinor's about Edward, it is quite untested; she knows, not by reason or argument, but by some kind of intuitive knowledge which she trusts. Jane Austen does not stop to ask if Marianne is justified, but the progress of the narrative will supply an answer.

Colonel Brandon's long account, which follows, of Willoughby's seduction of his ward throws a cold light on Willoughby's character and clears up the remaining mysteries of the first volume, bringing the initial impetus of the novel to a close. The hopes of Elinor and Marianne have come to nothing. Willoughby is married to a woman who can support him; Edward is to marry Lucy Steele; Colonel Brandon's story about Willoughby has brought no comfort. It is the nadir of the novel. Despite her suffering, Marianne is contemptuous of those who, like Mrs Jennings, do not have 'the delicacies of a strong sensibility, and the graces of a polished manner' (Chapter 31). In these words Marianne displays the close link she finds between her sensitivity and her sense of social superiority; her fine feelings border upon snobbery. And the narrator comments:

> Like half the rest of the world, if [no] more than half there be that are clever and good, Marianne, with excellent abilities and an excellent disposition, was neither reasonable nor candid. She expected from other people the same opinions and feelings as her own, and she judged of their motives by the immediate effect of their actions on herself. (*Chapter 31*)

Marianne's abilities and disposition are natural endowments; what she lacks are ways of regulating these qualities. To be 'reasonable' and 'candid' — a word Jane Austen uses in an older sense — means to be generous and comprehensive in one's judgments, applying an impersonal standard in a charitable way. Marianne is too self-centred to be just. The suggestion is that natural abilities are not sufficient in themselves to ensure the kind of behaviour of which Jane Austen approves: the large-minded impartiality of true virtue comes by discipline and effort.

For the moment the narrative pauses as the sisters deal as they can with the arrival of Mr and Mrs John Dashwood and the Steeles. They find they are treated less civilly than the Steeles, since Elinor is perceived as a danger to Edward whom his mother expects to marry well. Mrs John Dashwood, Lady Middleton and Mrs Ferrars establish themselves as leaders of the London season. Elinor and Marianne are condescended to, while the Steeles are taken up with enthusiasm. Elinor listens stonily to Mr Robert Ferrars's views on public schools and cottages. The second volume of *Sense and Sensibility* ends for the girls in banality and humiliation.

---

## Volume Three (*Chapters 37–50*)

---

When Anne Steele incautiously breaks the news of Lucy's engagement to Edward, Fanny Dashwood and Mrs Ferrars are outraged. Edward is banished, and his vain, self-complacent brother, Robert, is now to inherit Edward's share in his mother's estate. Edward and Lucy can now only look forward to a life of poverty in a country curacy. Colonel Brandon generously offers Edward a living which is in his gift. To her embarrassment the Colonel asks Elinor to tell Edward the good news. The two girls then leave London to visit the Palmers at their home in the country. There, as a result of her own impetuousness, Marianne falls ill. To Elinor's surprise, Willoughby arrives to inquire about her. He attempts to explain the circumstances which led to his break with Marianne and, although she cannot condone his conduct, Elinor is now able to judge him less harshly. When she is well enough, Marianne is also able to take stock of her own conduct during the affair; she has behaved selfishly. She has had no idea of the extent of Elinor's silent suffering over Edward Ferrars. Colonel Brandon now appears more attractive to the chastened Marianne. News is brought of the marriage between a Mr Ferrars and Lucy Steele. Everyone imagines she has married Edward Ferrars. In fact, she has married Edward's brother, Robert, as the Dashwoods learn when Edward arrives unexpectedly at Barton. Edward is now free to marry Elinor, and Marianne will marry Colonel Brandon.

Everything changes when Anne Steele is indiscreet enough to reveal that Lucy and Edward are secretly engaged. The revelation enables Marianne to see how differently from herself Elinor has behaved under her own disappointments. Their long dialogue in Chapter 37 serves to open Marianne's eyes to what her sister has had to suffer and how she has endured it. Elinor displays a further quality of the virtuous mind: she has by her own effort acquired a calm self-possession which is perhaps a necessary condition for the exercise of unselfish good will. For the moment she has to endure the renewed confidences of Lucy Steele and the embarrassment of being thought by Mrs Jennings to be about to marry Colonel Brandon, who then adds further embarrassment by asking her to convey to Edward the Colonel's offer of a rectory at his Delaford estate. She has to bear being told by her brother that now Mrs Ferrars regards her as less intolerable as a future daughter-in-law than Lucy Steele and that he, too, hopes she will marry Colonel Brandon. In this middle section of the novel her self-command is tested to its limit. Marianne is now fully aware of how differently her sister has behaved under circumstances similar to her own, but the knowledge has not yet begun to change her behaviour. Marianne's feelings are still focused entirely upon herself; she finds it impossible to exert herself to any exterior thoughts or activity, which Jane Austen appears to think essential for moral and psychological well-being. The removal of the sisters from London to Cleveland, as a first step on their journey home, announces the end of a lustreless episode: London has not been kind to them. Before she leaves, Elinor duly carries out the task of offering Edward Ferrars the rectory at Delaford which will be a small means of livelihood for him. The last barrier to his marriage with Lucy Steele has been removed.

At Cleveland, Mrs Palmer's house, Marianne's fever, brought about by her own thoughtlessness, brings the action of the novel to a crisis. Willoughby returns with his own explanation of the behaviour which so diminished his reputation in the eyes of Marianne's friends (Chapter 44). In this scene Jane Austen justifies Marianne's intuitive belief that Willoughby was not wholly to blame for what had happened. It was indeed true that the letter which had ended their friendship had been dictated by the woman who was to become his wife. But the reader is left to make the connection for himself: does the fact itself serve — at least in part — to justify Marianne's intuition, and does Jane Austen mean us to believe that it does? Is she implying that sensibility can sometimes provide knowledge which is beyond the reach of sense, or is she simply providing a rather lame excuse for Willoughby's behaviour?

Jane Austen handles the episodes at Cleveland in a style that touches upon melodrama. Of course, the reader must exercise some sympathetic historical imagination to recall a time when a 'putrid sore throat' was the symptom of many infections some of which, under the medical supervision then available, might be fatal. More puzzling is the treatment of Willoughby, who is even allowed to imply that Colonel Brandon may not have told the whole truth when he accused Willoughby of seducing Eliza, the Colonel's ward. Is the aim of this scene to justify Willoughby, or to justify Marianne's love for him? Willoughby's language of passion — as he himself admits — is expressed in 'hackneyed metaphor', and it is difficult to accept that he did not know that the girl he had abandoned was in want simply because he had forgotten to give her his address. We are only too aware of the exaggeration of melodrama when we read of Willoughby, torn between Marianne, 'beautiful as an angel' and Sophia the woman he marries 'jealous as the devil', or of Mrs Smith, his cousin, whose life alone stands between Willoughby and wealth, forcing him by her rigid morality to give up his expectations of wealth from her and to seek it in the woman to whom he is now miserably married. For a moment, at least, Elinor is taken in by his sophisticated but tawdry rhetoric. She even has to concede that there is something about Willoughby's physical presence that almost persuades her to excuse his weakness of character. Elinor's fixed sentiment of abhorrence for Willoughby has been modified by pity for his suffering, even though it has been the consequence of his own folly. But she is aware of the influence of his good looks and pleasant manner, though none of these qualities has any moral value. Even his feeling for Marianne ought to be held against him now that he is married. But Elinor has to acknowledge that her involuntary sympathy for him will not easily fade from her mind. The tension between sympathy and reason is expressed here with some force, though it is not examined in detail. Neither Elinor nor her creator allow themselves to go beyond the boundary of the rational and to examine the claims of these troubling sympathies and affections. But they do pay tribute to their strength.

Willoughby's departure is followed by the arrival of Mrs Dashwood, who now believes that Colonel Brandon will be a more suitable partner for Marianne. Their return home brings Marianne to a calmer frame of mind. She acknowledges how selfish she has been, and the process of reformation begins. When Elinor tells Marianne about Willoughby's visit, her sympathy for him is less evident than it was during his visit:

> Reflection had given calmness to her judgement, and sobered her . . . opinion of Willoughby's desert; — she wished, therefore, to declare only the simple truth, and lay open such facts as were really due to his character, without any embellishment of tenderness to lead the fancy astray. (*Chapter 47*)

Only three chapters separate this account of Elinor's feelings from the description given previously. Then, under Willoughby's immediate influence, the truth was not so simple. Then her tender feelings were less easily separated from her judgment. Jane Austen has allowed for the force of natural feelings, but they are not to be judged to be good because they are natural. They are subject to the scrutiny of reason according to the standard of what is right. Now her judgment is severe, as she tells Marianne:

> 'It was selfishness which first made him sport with your affections; which afterwards, when his own were engaged, made him delay the confession of it, and which finally carried him from Barton. His own enjoyment, or his own ease, was, in every particular, his ruling principle.' (*Chapter 47*)

Willoughby disposed of, and Marianne's eyes opened, there remains the matter of Edward. A servant reports that Lucy Steele and Mr Ferrars are married. But Edward's arrival clears the matter up: it is *Robert* Ferrars whom Lucy has married. If some readers are surprised at the unexpected alliance between Robert Ferrars and Lucy Steele, they may wish to compare the account given of their acquaintance in Chapter 49 with what Robert Ferrars tells Elinor about Lucy in Chapter 27. It is rather difficult to believe that a man like Robert, so self-centred and so careful of his reputation, would be likely to fall in love with Lucy Steele. But readers will have to judge for themselves how convincing they find the resolution of this final mystery in the novel. A partial reconciliation with his mother allows Edward to marry Elinor, and John Dashwood now encourages Elinor to find some way of bringing Marianne and Colonel Brandon together. Marianne's conversion is now complete. She has had to learn that life is not best regulated by feeling and that second thoughts may be best. Jane Austen ends her account of these crucial events in the life of Marianne in a way that may remind the reader of the opening paragraphs of *Northanger Abbey*. Marianne has not conformed to the conventional image of the heroine of fiction; having narrated her painful story, Jane Austen can now treat her with irony:

Marianne Dashwood was born to an extraordinary fate. She was born to discover the falsehood of her own opinions, and to counteract, by her conduct, her most favourite maxims. She was born to overcome an affection formed so late in life as at seventeen, and with no sentiment superior to strong esteem and lively friendship, voluntarily to give her hand to another! — and *that* other, a man who had suffered no less than herself under the event of a former attachment, whom, two years before, she had considered too old to be married, — and who still sought the constitutional safeguard of a flannel waistcoat.

But so it was. Instead of falling sacrifice to an irresistible passion, as once she had fondly flattered herself with expecting — she found herself at nineteen, submitting to new attachments, entering on new duties, placed in a new home, a wife, the mistress of a family, and the patroness of a village. (*Chapter 50*)

Jane Austen's irony plays on the conventions of romance until their insubstantiality is revealed. But they have at least the justification of being the assumptions of youth. In this paragraph we can see the transformation brought about by the perception that there is a continuity of experience between youth and middle-age, and that the time-scale of affection may be longer than that of passion. In the last sentence, Jane Austen's irony gives way to a celebration of 'the common feelings of common life', as she puts it in *Northanger Abbey*. Compared with the responsibilities that the young women of Jane Austen's novels — and of her time — might look forward to, Marianne's initial expectations seem trivial. Her own selfishness had been no less deep-rooted than Willoughby's. Thanks to the guidance and example of Elinor, she has made her way to an active social position where sensibility will be properly regulated by good sense.

# Conclusion

Superficially, the title of the novel may appear to imply that 'sense' and 'sensibility' are simply opposed to one another. But this is not so. Although 'sense' refers to a single concept, even if it appears under the names of 'judgment' or 'reason', 'sensibility' has a number of meanings. Marianne Dashwood's sensibility is essentially aesthetic. (Think of her address to Norland and its trees at the beginning of Chapter 5, and her keen pleasure in the 'high downs' and 'animating gales' of Barton.) Her impetuous and absolute feelings take the place of judgment. She does not expect to question what she feels. Her mother displays some of the same characteristics. As she says, 'I have never yet known what it was to separate esteem and love' (Chapter 3). And when Elinor speaks of her feeling for Edward in terms of 'liking' and 'esteem' (Chapter 4), Marianne says, 'Esteem him! Like Him! Cold-hearted Elinor! . . . Use these words again and I will leave the room this moment!' (This outburst is worth comparing with the narrator's summing up of Marianne previously quoted.) For Marianne and Mrs Dashwood, affection has no gradations. It is never illuminated by thoughtful assessment. Mere receptiveness to feelings is not valuable in itself if it is unaccompanied by moral perceptiveness. Too often, as the example of Marianne shows, cultivating 'feelings' goes along with a preoccupation with self. Mrs John Dashwood and Mrs Ferrars, for example, are credited with a sensibility which is purely self-regarding. As Fanny and John Dashwood show, selfishness can be uncoloured by aesthetic feeling of any sort. Their only preoccupation is their own well-being. Another example of this kind of selfishness is the indifference of Lady Middleton to everything except the empty social conventions which occupy her attention.

Jane Austen does not mean to diminish our respect for feeling, but she does want to distinguish between valuable and less valuable feeling. True feeling sympathises with the distress of others. Sir John Middleton displays this feeling towards Willoughby, when it is said of him, 'His heart was softened by seeing him [Willoughby] suffer.' Mrs Jennings displays it towards Marianne, as well as to her daughter, Charlotte, giving her practical help when her baby is born. It is perhaps characteristic of the limitations of Marianne's sensibility that she says of Mrs Jennings, 'She cannot feel. Her kindness is no sympathy; her good nature is not tenderness' (Chapter 31). We are reminded that for Marianne 'the delicacies of a strong sensibility' — notice the irony of that collocation of 'delicate' and 'strong' — go hand-in-hand with 'the graces of a polished manner.' There is a danger that Marianne's aesthetic sensibility is too closely allied to the cold hearted complacency of Mrs John Dashwood or Lady Middleton or the foppishness of Robert Ferrars who spends a quarter of an hour examining and debating over every toothpick in Gray's shop.

Jane Austen, as we have seen, goes to considerable lengths to establish that feeling is not disregarded by Elinor; she is perfectly well aware of its strength. But for her, feeling must be subordinated to a self-command which is regulated by a moral understanding based on reason. 'Moral understanding' appears to include an awareness of one's place in the world and how much one may reasonably expect of life. If it is submissive, it is a submission of the mind to a reality external to itself. A woman in Elinor's position has fairly narrow expectations. Unless she has a private income, she is totally dependant on other people. There is no suggestion in the novel that the Dashwood girls should earn their own living. Their only resource is marriage. If they do not marry, they will be obliged to live with their mother on the resources which she has, and on the charity of their brother — or of such friends as Sir John Middleton, who provides the widowed Mrs Dashwood with a cottage far less luxurious and spacious than the cottage which Mr Robert Ferrars imagines would be big enough to hold a dance in and which would contain a dining-parlour, a drawing room, a library and a saloon. The Dashwoods in their cottage at Barton Park may well remind us of Jane Austen's own situation at Chawton. Jane Austen knew from personal experience what it was like to be the dependant daughter of a clergyman; she knew, too, what it was like to have her old home taken over by an elder brother. Elinor Dashwood knows that she cannot afford to regulate her conduct by feeling. For her, the main function of sympathetic feeling is to see things from another's point of view. Her moral understanding proceeds from a sense of duty which imposes absolute commands upon her to behave towards others as she would have them behave to her. There is an obligation, too, to avoid harming others, to keep promises, to keep her troubles to herself, and to make constant efforts to look outwards. Her imagination never wastes its energy in fantasy; it is at the service of a disciplined attempt to see the events of her life truthfully and comprehensively.

# Chapter 4

# Pride and Prejudice:
## knowing others

## Introduction

*Pride and Prejudice* is essentially concerned with a small group of characters who constitute the core of the novel. The novel is grounded in the contrasted fortunes of two sisters: the central intertwining strands of its narrative trace how Elizabeth and Jane Bennet arrive at suitable marriages with
men whose characters and affections they can be sure of, and who will be
able to offer them a satisfying life of shared interests and mutual love.
Among the central themes of the novel are the questions of what love is and
how it can be recognised. But a prior question is how it is possible to gain
dependable knowledge of other people, given the complexity of human
character and motive and the number of accidents by which life is affected.

## Commentary

**Volume One (*Chapters 1–23*)**

In the first chapters of the novel the theme of knowledge is rapidly developed. Gaining knowledge of others is quite different from the book-learning
Mary Bennet prides herself on: it is an aspect of general intelligence, which
is not distributed equally among Jane Austen's characters. Having shown
us, for example, the disparity between Mr and Mrs Bennet through the
conversation which occupies most of Chapter 1, she says of Mrs Bennet:

> She was a woman of mean understanding, little information, and uncer-
> tain temper. When she was discontented she fancied herself nervous.
> The business of her life was to get her daughters married; its solace was
> visiting and news.

Mr and Mrs Bennet's incompatibility of mind and character is the element in which their family has been nurtured. Her obtuse and petty prac-
ticality has blunted the edge of his good temper. His wit sometimes betrays
indifference to the real welfare of his family; his perversity is sometimes

almost cruel. His withdrawal into the library prevents him from exercising the paternal care his daughters surely require.

Real knowledge of others is not easily acquired in Longbourn. The formality of social custom prevents Mr Bingley from seeing the sisters when he calls on their father. Opinion in the village is easily formed and as easily changed: the approval of Darcy's good looks changes when he is discovered to be proud. Elizabeth Bennet has her own reason for disliking him. He has too rapidly decided that only Jane is worth looking at, and has consequently snubbed Elizabeth. Mrs Bennet's judgment of him echoes the general judgment of Longbourn:

> ' . . . he is a most disagreeable, horrid man, not at all worth pleasing. So high and conceited that there was no enduring him! He walked here, and he walked there, fancying himself so very great! . . . I quite detest the man.' (*Chapter 3*)

When Jane and Elizabeth talk together alone, they display a more penetrating capacity for judging others, but there are significant differences between them. Elizabeth relies on her intelligence to reach a conclusion — not always charitable — about the people she meets. Jane, on the other hand, is a woman of instinctive goodness; her goodwill towards others is such that it sees only their virtues and refuses to see anything bad. Such generosity may be mistaken. Jane Austen contrasts the judgments of the Bingley sisters in a sentence which reveals the author's own capacity for discriminating analysis:

> . . . with more quickness of observation and less pliancy of temper than her sister, and with a judgment too unassailed by any attention to herself, [Elizabeth] was very little disposed to approve of them [Miss Bingley and Mrs Hurst]. (*Chapter 4*)

Elizabeth's capacity for judgment is composed of a mixture of qualities: she sees more than Jane, but she is less willing to be pleased with what she sees. These qualities serve her well if they have not been seduced by some flattering attention which might sway her. The narrative voice confirms Elizabeth's judgment of Mr Bingley's sisters when it goes on authoritatively, 'They were in fact very fine ladies . . . ' The narrator is using exactly those techniques of rational analysis which Elizabeth has used, but the character is not yet credited with the narrator's infallibility.

The tone of the narrative commentary — incisive, assured and exact — provides a clue to the general strategy which Jane Austen adopts in this novel. There is a mixture in it of fixed and of open elements. Its central situation — the relationship which develops between Elizabeth and Darcy — depends on chance and uncertainty. Initially, the nature of the characters is not entirely clear, but since the novel is presented in part from Elizabeth's point of view, we are given privileged access to her suspicions. The character of

Darcy is deliberately hidden from us, as it is from Elizabeth. As she is contrasted with Jane, as a character in development as opposed to one formed in goodness, so Darcy is contrasted with Bingley, the 'easiness' and 'openness' of the latter apparently at odds with Darcy's fastidious reserve. The pliancy of Jane's temper matches the ductility of Bingley's. There is no such initial consistency between Elizabeth and Darcy, but one fact firmly established by the narrator modifies our view of Darcy: he admires Bingley and Bingley admires him in return. The fact that Elizabeth and Darcy are responsive to established types of goodness helps us to modify our impression of her as merely 'witty' and of Darcy as merely 'proud': beneath the surface wit of the former and the formality of the latter lies a common attachment to characters who are good. Even as early as the fourth chapter of the novel we begin to see the characters ranged on scales of intellectual and moral excellence. Mary — for all her book-learning — Kitty, Lydia and Mrs Bennet rank low on the first of these; Elizabeth and her father rate much more highly. But it is not clear that intelligence and virtue are highly correlated.

There is a third scale of values which matters to the characters of the novel: it is, of course, the scale of social class, based on rank or wealth. The Bennet's neighbours, the Lucases, owe their position to success in business, but Sir William Lucas has abandoned both his business, and the place where he conducted it, in favour of Lucas Lodge, 'where he could think with pleasure of his own importance, and unshackled by business, occupy himself wholly in being civil to all the world' (Chapter 5). But despite his appearance at the Court of St James's, Sir William occupies a lowly place on the ladder of rank, at the top of which is to be found Darcy's aunt, Lady Catherine de Bourgh. Ranged upon it, and judging their success in life solely with reference to it, are Bingley's sisters, Mr Collins, Charlotte Lucas and Mrs Bennet.

Within these larger questions of values is set the question of marriage. The famous opening sentence of the novel ironically characterises marriage as an institution for supplying masculine needs. Mothers and daughters have a commodity to supply: Mrs Bennet's haste to use the convention of the social call to put her in touch with a man to whom she can be of service does not appear to her odd or improper. Charlotte Lucas, who has her father's admiration for social position, has no other means of obtaining it than by marriage. Her attitude to the institution is straightforward: sexual preferences may be unpredictable, but once they show themselves, they should be nurtured. According to Charlotte, so far as Bingley is concerned,

> Jane should . . . make the most of every half hour in which she can command his attention. When she is secure of him, there will be leisure for falling in love as much as she chooses. (*Chapter 6*)

Charlotte sees marriage as a question of the enticement and capture of the man by the woman. She is entirely cynical about the need to know the character of one's marriage partner:

> Happiness in marriage is entirely a matter of chance. If the dispositions of the parties are ever so well known to each other, or ever so similar before-hand, it does not advance their felicity in the least. (*Chapter 6*)

There is a brittle cynicism about this paragraph. It is witty and cleverly turned, but it shows little sign of the pressure of experience. Elizabeth does not believe Charlotte would ever act in this way herself. But she does.

The wooing of Charlotte brings the first volume of the novel to an end, hinting at the uncertainty of the future of the Bennet girls when their father dies. Charlotte has accepted marriage as a means of security, but Elizabeth regards the match with regret; in her eyes Charlotte has 'sacrificed every better feeling to worldly advantage' (Chapter 22). She does not believe that such degradation can lead to happiness.

The more complex ideas of marriage presented in the novel demand a more leisurely presentation. The love affair between Jane Bennet and Bingley is direct and uncomplicated, the attraction of two handsome and well-matched people, who are generous and open-hearted. The main interest of their story is whether the jealousy of Mr Bingley's sisters and Darcy's disapproval will keep them apart. The relationship which develops between Elizabeth and Darcy is much more complex—too complex, perhaps, for Jane Austen to handle with complete success at this stage of her writing career. The task she undertakes is immense: Darcy is the most differentiated male character she ever attempted; he is intelligent, sensitive, aloof, keenly conscious of the dignity of his social position, and strongly attracted to beautiful women. He is embarrassed when he falls in love with a girl of Elizabeth's unpromising family connections. Such a figure might be a subject for comedy, but Jane Austen means us to be sympathetic to his fastidiousness. Elizabeth comes to see that her first impressions of him have been wrong. Besides attempting to portray this strong but enigmatic male figure, she records the complicated process of self-evaluation which both Darcy and Elizabeth undergo. With Elizabeth her task is simpler, since we can share her experiences and overhear her reflections upon them. Darcy's thoughts are hidden both from Elizabeth and from the reader: like her, we can observe his actions, but we do not immediately understand his motives or his purposes. The transformation of their relationship from misunderstanding to witty flirtatiousness, and then to rational love is prolonged and far from straightforward; indeed, not all the doubts we may have about Darcy's character are resolved. The wit and comic inventiveness of the novel are undeniable, but has Jane Austen successfully conveyed her central characters' changing perceptions? To answer this question, we must return to the text.

At Netherfield Elizabeth runs the gauntlet of the malice of Miss Bingley and Mrs Hurst. She is made a testing-ground for the value-systems there. Charles Bingley admires her sisterly affection and her agreeableness. His sisters stress her low connections and censure her for walking through the mud to visit Jane. When Elizabeth rejoins the party, Jane Austen begins to tighten the threads which link her to Darcy: she likes reading; he is always buying books. As is her custom, Jane Austen brings them closer through animated talk. As the conversation grows warm on the accomplishments of women, it becomes a dialogue between Elizabeth and Darcy. His requirements of women become so excessive that Elizabeth doubts if they can ever be met. The Bingley sisters protest against her suggestion that few, if any, women meet his criteria, clearly believing they qualify themselves. But Darcy snubs Miss Bingley with a hint that her accomplishments are principally used to capture male attention.

When Mrs Bennet arrives at Netherfield to visit Jane, Darcy's patience and Elizabeth's resourcefulness are strained. She does her best to mitigate the effect of her mother's stupid rudeness, but Mrs Bennet's behaviour has partly justified the Bingley sisters' disdain for Elizabeth's relatives. Whatever effect the visit has on Mr Darcy's opinion of Elizabeth, it does not improve his impression of Caroline Bingley. Despite his rebuff, she continues her advances with ill-considered remarks about the letter-writing he is engaged upon, but her attempts to ingratiate herself with him by complimenting his sister fall flat. Once more Jane Austen works through conversation to move from the trivial to the complex. Now the talk is of personal attitudes and character — in particular, Charles Bingley's wish to represent himself as careless and impetuous. As it becomes sharper and more personal, Elizabeth joins in. It begins to be a dispute about the relative claims of sentiment and logic, with Elizabeth defending the first, Darcy the second. The point of the talk is the value of friendship: Bingley wants to boast of his own rashness; Darcy wants to persuade him of his willingness to please. Which is the better man — he who rigidly adheres to his own purposes, or he who yields to the persuasion of a friend? The talk is rapid, jocular and inconclusive. Elizabeth and Darcy revel in argument but to Bingley an argument is 'too like a dispute' for comfort.

The climax of this series of conversations begins on the evening when Jane is well enough to join the rest of the party and enjoy the attentions of Charles Bingley. Caroline Bingley's efforts to endear herself to Mr Darcy by aping his interest in books are ineffective; she does not impress by pretending to prefer the pleasures of conversation to those of dancing. She is reduced to walking about the room to win his attention, but she wins it only when Elizabeth joins her. Once again, initial conversational commonplaces exchanged within the group lead to a witty exchange between Elizabeth and Darcy (Chapter 11). It begins with Miss Bingley's assertion that Darcy is not to be laughed at. Elizabeth is sceptical about Darcy's immunity from ridicule; he counters by saying that anyone may become the victim of a determined joker. Her insistence that she would laugh only at 'follies and nonsense, whim and inconsistencies' leads to her daring to specify two weaknesses—vanity and pride—from which he may suffer. He accepts that vanity would be a weakness, but that 'where there is real superiority of mind, pride will be always under good regulation'. The superiority of mind in which he takes pride is sufficient to allow Elizabeth to smile at him, though she is careful to hide it. Evidently Darcy thinks he has no faults. He does not think he is short of intelligence, though he may have faults of temper. Perhaps he is liable not to change his mind, if he has formed an opinion against someone:

' . . . I cannot forget the follies and vices of others so soon as I ought, nor their offences against myself. My feelings are not puffed about with every attempt to move them. My temper would perhaps be called resentful. — My good opinion once lost is lost for ever.' (*Chapter 11*)

Here, then is the unyielding man whom they have previously discussed. The conversation of the previous evening had been broken off when Charles Bingley had hinted at a touch of moroseness in Darcy's temper. Now the account Darcy has given of himself goes beyond anything Elizabeth can laugh at. Beneath the cut and thrust of their debate we can sense that she is genuinely shocked. The charge of relentlessness which he has made against himself will stay in her mind when she hears more about Darcy from Wickham, who arrives in Longbourn as a young officer in the militia. These conversations at Netherfield have brought Elizabeth and Darcy closer, but we cannot assume that they have formed accurate impressions of one another.

The story of Wickham and his association with Darcy is set within the story of Mr Collins's quest for a bride. Both characters are linked with the central action of the novel through their connection with Darcy: Mr Collins is the subservient chaplain to Mr Darcy's imperious aunt; Wickham has had expectations of advancement through Darcy's late father which have been mysteriously thwarted. Mr Collins's revelation that Lady Catherine expects Darcy to marry her daughter provides a new possibility for the outcome of events, dashing Miss Bingley's hopes of Darcy and edging him from Elizabeth's attention, which now focuses on Wickham. She accepts his account of Darcy's injustice to him, and finds in his accusation support for her belief in Darcy's unattractive rigidity of temper. But Elizabeth's assessment of Wickham's character (which she shares with her very impressionable sisters, Lydia and Kitty) is based on his 'fine countenance', his 'good figure' and his 'very pleasing address' (Chapter 15). Elizabeth will have cause later in the novel to look back on these first impressions and wonder what evidence his appearance could have given her of his trustworthiness.

The tension between Wickham and Darcy, evident at their first embarrassed meeting, is the public sign of something mysterious about their relationship which is gradually unfolded as the action of the novel develops. Elizabeth's fate, it may be said, depends on which of these men she chooses to believe. Wickham's account of his dealings with Darcy coincides with her own view of Darcy's character and she accepts it at face value, despite some evidence that there might be truth in Darcy's assertion that Wickham had forfeited his claim to the preferment promised him by his father. Wickham admits to having 'a warm unguarded temper' (Chapter 16) but he confesses to no more than verbal aggression against Darcy. Elizabeth is content to accept Wickham's view that he and Darcy 'are very different sort of men, and that he hates me.' When she searches for a motive for Darcy's dislike, Wickham suggests jealousy. When she pauses for a moment, doubting that Darcy can be as bad as Wickham says, Darcy's words at Netherfield come back to her and she recalls him 'boasting . . . of the implacability of his resentments, of his having an unforgiving temper.' Twice in the course of her dialogue with Wickham, Elizabeth is credited with an awareness of his good looks, and Jane Austen follows her unspoken thought when she wonders how Darcy could have treated so badly 'a young man . . . like *you*, whose very countenance may vouch for your being amiable.' The astounding nature of Wickham's tale makes Darcy appear 'abominable'. In Wickham's view, Darcy is corroded by family pride, and his sister is as proud as he is. Mr Collins's account of Lady Catherine de Bourgh only adds one more touch to the picture Elizabeth has formed of an arrogant and conceited family. Jane agrees with her that it is not possible 'to question the veracity of a young man of such amiable appearance as Wickham', but both are puzzled by the fact that a man of such a disagreeable nature can impose upon Mr Bingley.

The last chapters of the first volume are more relaxed. They deal with the frankly comic episodes of Mr Collins's proposal to Elizabeth. The clergyman's foolishness is thoroughly exposed by his use of language. Its amplitude, its precise particularity, its complacent condescension are irresistibly funny. Mr Collins lacks any self-appraisal; he has neither humility nor self-awareness. He is deliciously self-absorbed. Consider the bait he unctuously offers Elizabeth to join him as the wife of Lady Catherine's sedulous retainer:

> 'Allow me, by the way, to observe, my fair cousin, that I do not reckon the notice and kindness of Lady Catherine de Bourgh as among the least of the advantages in my power to offer. You will find her manners beyond any thing I can describe; and your wit and vivacity I think must be acceptable to her, especially when tempered with the silence and respect which her rank will inevitably excite.' (*Chapter 19*)

We know enough of Elizabeth's independence of mind to surmise how she will receive Mr Collins's remarks. Respect and silence are scarcely compatible with wit and vivacity, and Elizabeth is not awed by rank. She is not likely to take kindly to the idea that marriage to Mr Collins would confer a favour upon her. But it is not at all surprising that he cannot understand Elizabeth's succinct refusal. Jane Austen prolongs the comic confusion with the help of Mrs Bennet, but she has already prepared a more receptive ear for the insistent clergyman. Charlotte Lucas has helped to relieve Elizabeth of Mr Collins's attentions at the Netherfield ball; her criteria for a marriage-partner have already been explored; it is not difficult for us to believe that she would be prepared to accept him as a husband.

The engagement of Mr Collins and Charlotte Lucas provides the sense of an ending to a sequence of episodes which leave many unanswered questions. The encounters between Elizabeth and Darcy have suggested possibilities of relationship which are still to be explored; these characters have begun to talk to one another in language which suggests emotional depth and intellectual engagement. The abjectness of Charlotte's acceptance of Mr Collins throws into relief the unromantic plight of the unmarried middle-class girl without independent means, but Mr Collins himself is presented through the language he uses as a figure near to parody. He is a brilliant creation but may well be thought as ill-matched artistically with Charlotte as he is in other ways. Bingley's sudden disappearance from Netherfield may be consistent with the impression he has given, but is it consistent with the character Jane Bennet has come to know and love?

## Volume Two (*Chapters 24–42*)

The second volume begins with Jane Bennet's growing belief that Bingley, influenced by the opinion of his friends, has deserted her. Jane accepts the situation with fortitude. She suffers, but she shows no pain, nor does she blame Bingley. It is Elizabeth who is despondent enough to say:

'The more I see of the world, the more I am dissatisfied with it; and every day confirms my belief of the inconsistency of all human characters, and of the little dependence that can be placed on the appearance of either merit or sense.' (*Chapter 24*).

If Jane Bennet has an unceasing faith in the goodness and honesty of those she encounters, Elizabeth's opinion here is close to despair. It appears to be supported by Bingley's defection and by Charlotte Lucas's mercenary marriage. Jane opposes her sister's bleak views of human nature with a charitable good sense which is based on two propositions—first, that the world is much more governed by chance than we might suppose; and, second, that it is nevertheless intelligible. To believe that she has been the object of a conspiracy by Bingley's friends would be painful; it is better to believe she was mistaken about the strength of his affection.

For a very brief period, Jane Austen plays with the idea that Wickham might be in love with Elizabeth, a suggestion originally made by Mr Bennet in a characteristically quizzical phrase, as unhelpful as it is uncommitted. It is at this point that Elizabeth's aunt, Mrs Gardiner, arrives on a visit from London; she is a civilised, sensible woman, despite the fact that she lives in an unfashionable part of London and has a husband who 'lived by trade' (Chapter 25). (We may, of course, suspect that these descriptions are meant to recommend her.) She warns Elizabeth against falling in love with a man with no money, but she admits Wickham's charm, and is prejudiced in his favour because she knows and loves the part of the county where he was brought up. Darcy, of course, had been brought up there too, and Jane Austen will use this contact between Mrs Gardiner and Derbyshire as part of the machinery of her plot.

Immediate contact with Wickham is soon broken. Elizabeth admits his attractiveness, but goes no further. Soon, however, she has to report that Wickham has transfered his affections to a girl who has just inherited money. Elizabeth has not been deeply enough involved with Wickham to be affected by his behaviour. Her concern is with Jane, who, having returned to London with her aunt, is now the recipient of Miss Bingley's chilly friendship. Now, even Jane has to admit that she has been mistaken about Miss Bingley: she even begins to believe that Bingley has deceived her, but she endeavours to 'banish every painful thought, and think only of what will make me happy, [Elizabeth's] affection, and the invariable kindness of my dear uncle and aunt' (Chapter 26). Meanwhile, Elizabeth, sustained only by her aunt's promise to include her in a tour to the Lake District, prepares to visit the new Mrs Collins. Later in the novel it becomes clearer what use Jane Austen is making of Mrs Gardiner as a means of unravelling some of the knots she has deliberately introduced into her plot. The mention of the Lake District is part of a false trail that leads back to Derbyshire, as we shall see, and Mrs Gardiner is an essential part of a rather awkward structural device for bringing separated lovers together.

Elizabeth's visit to the Collinses at Hunsford allows her to continue her acquaintance with Darcy. Their meetings are public and their conversations have an oblique, teasing quality which is not without intimacy. Elizabeth compares the stiffness of his manners with the stiffness of her fingers at the keyboard: both come from lack of practice and neither can escape the blame of not having taken enough trouble to learn. Darcy does not accept the description as true of her, and side-steps her criticism with a remark which hints at a new level of intimacy between them:

> 'You are perfectly right. You have employed your time much better. No one admitted to the privilege of hearing you, can think anything wanting. We neither of us perform to strangers.' (*Chapter 31*)

The warmth of the remark—its suggestion of an acknowledged relationship between them—is not consciously registered by Elizabeth, though she now no longer believes Darcy is interested in Miss De Bourgh; as she puts it, 'he might have been just as likely to marry *her*, had she been his relation' (Chapter 31). More clues are offered about Mr Darcy's feelings for Elizabeth, though no direct expression of them is allowed, though Charlotte Collins comments on the visit Darcy makes to the Parsonage and notices the 'earnest steadfast gaze' (Chapter 32) with which he regards Elizabeth.

The clearest indication of Mr Darcy's feelings about Elizabeth are revealed by the characteristically confused conversation they have about the value of local attachments; she thinks he has caught her thinking how convenient it would have been for Jane, if Mr Bingley had remained at Netherfield; in fact, we may suspect he is wondering how Elizabeth would react to being taken away from her family at Longbourn. As he moves his chair nearer to her, we expect the sense of intimacy to be expressed in words, but Elizabeth draws back, and he does the same. His remarks about her connections with Longbourn are obscure enough to surprise her, but they certainly imply she is too good to be merely the product of a country village.

Although the narrative abounds with evidence of the strength of Darcy's interest in Elizabeth, Jane Austen deliberately keeps Elizabeth unaware of it. Even the clear-sighted Charlotte cannot quite decide whether Darcy's behaviour signifies love or boredom: even the 'earnest steadfast gaze' may be mere absence of mind. Elizabeth's mind is too clouded by prejudice to suspect a motive behind the frequency with which he just happens to meet her on her walks. Darcy does not know that his reputation has suffered another blow when his cousin, Colonel Fitzwilliam, says enough to make Elizabeth suspect it has been Darcy who brought about Bingley's separation from Jane. Colonel Fitzwilliam does not know the effect of his report that Darcy had congratulated himself on saving a friend from an imprudent marriage, but it gives Elizabeth pain. Darcy may despise the modest social station of the Bennets and their relations but (as Elizabeth puts it to herself), 'To Jane herself . . . there could be no possibility of objection. All loveliness and goodness as she is!' (Chapter 32). To the evident fact of Jane's beauty and goodness Elizabeth has attached some half-truths about her father and some unsupported suppositions about Darcy's values and intentions. She underestimates his distaste for Mrs Bennet's behaviour which has often made Elizabeth uneasy. The key to Darcy's character, she believes, is snobbery: it is 'this worst kind of pride' (Chapter 33) of which she believes him guilty. As she is in this state of angry distress, reinforced by a reading of Jane's sad letters to her, he appears to tell her how much he loves her.

Elizabeth's rejection of Darcy's proposal is presented with the greatest possible energy: it is the climax of their cross-purposes, each seeing the other in the worst possible light, each convinced of personal rectitude. Darcy has no compunction about confessing the sense of degradation he feels in telling Elizabeth that he loves her; he even expects her to understand his pleasure in helping Bingley not to do what he has just done himself. He cannot understand that he has wounded her and made her angry. Up to this point Elizabeth and Darcy have been curiously insulated from each other; however close to intimacy they may have come, they have not understood each other's feelings. Elizabeth's account of the pain he has caused her through his behaviour to Jane and to Wickham is forceful, closely reasoned and controlled, culminating in her calmly contemptuous assurance, 'You could not have made me the offer of your hand in any possible way that would have tempted me to accept it' (Chapter 34). Her summary of her feelings towards him is unrelenting in its resolute dislike and Darcy retreats with as much wounded dignity as he can muster. Left to herself, her feelings are more mixed. Jane Austen's expression of them beautifully conveys the flood of new feelings by which Elizabeth is assailed and their recoil against the judgment she has formed about Darcy's defects of character. Now she can contemplate more calmly his prejudice against her which has been finally undermined by his affection. Her knowledge of the strength of the prejudice allows her to estimate how strong his love has been. Yet those prejudices injured Jane, and, in addition, he has been cruel to Wickham. Jane Austen has no difficulty in persuading us that Elizabeth's principal feelings are of anger and resentment, but we now know that she has been given a new view of Darcy and that new feelings may be attached to it.

Jane Austen now attempts to rehabilitate Darcy by the letter of self-justification he hands to Elizabeth the next day. Her first problem is to deal with Darcy's heartless treatment of Jane, which must implicate Bingley, who has yielded to his pressure. In Darcy's defence she uses Jane's unruffled good temper which allows him to plead ignorance of Jane's affection for Bingley. All he was aware of was the gossip about their possible marriage and Mrs Bennet's unattractive efforts to bring it about. It is less easy for us to believe in Darcy's ignorance about Jane's feelings, since we know so much about them, but we must remember Jane's own scrupulous restraint, commented upon so adversely by Charlotte Lucas. While Bingley may appear to have accepted Darcy's opinion too easily (is this the defect of the sweetness of temper Elizabeth earlier commended?), he cannot be accused of not wanting to see Jane again. That he does not know Jane is in London helps to account for his failure to do so.

Jane Austen does not attempt to conceal Darcy's sense of social superiority but is it the simple snobbery Elizabeth believes it to be? The narrator's description of Mrs Bennet's tactlessness, Lydia's impertinence and Mary's foolish self-aggrandisement has been pointed enough to justify Darcy's criticism. Elizabeth knows her family's faults; it is perhaps a matter for debate whether Darcy is right to be so aware of them, though his public insistence on them is tactless. About Elizabeth's accusations concerning

Wickham, Darcy is precise and circumstantial. If his story is correct, Wickham's behaviour has been wicked and deceitful. And Elizabeth has been deceived.

In Chapter 36, Jane Austen traces the process of reinterpretation which goes on in Elizabeth's mind when she considers the force of Darcy's argument. At first, her anger is renewed, but his account of Wickham's behaviour is too detailed to be ignored. She tries to believe that 'on both sides it was only assertion', but the details begin to persuade her that Darcy may have been 'blameless throughout'. Now she realises that she knows nothing about Wickham except what he has told her. The old-fashioned formality of the language in which Wickham's behaviour is analysed cannot hide, and in many ways enhances the fact, that she has had to take account of the extraordinary force of simple sexual attraction. Memory helps Elizabeth Bennet to see what kind of character lies beneath Wickham's appearance: in its light she can see how precipitate Wickham has been in telling her about his personal life; how bold his words about Darcy have been, compared to his actions; how easy he had found it to depreciate Darcy; how quickly he had been attracted to the modest fortune of Miss King. She sees Darcy now in a different light, and suffers a sudden revulsion against herself:

> 'How despicably have I acted', she cried—'I, who have prided myself on my discernment'.—I, who have valued myself on my abilities! who have often disdained the generous candour of my sister, and gratified my vanity, in useless or blameable distrust.—How humiliating is this discovery! Yet how just a humiliation!' (*Chapter 36*)

It is worth comparing this turn in the plot—this moment of self-recognition—with a similar, but more richly particularised and more cunningly engineered, episode in *Emma*. It is also essential to remember that the word 'candour' here means a generous willingness to believe the best of people.

When the Bennet girls return to Longbourn they are soon plunged into the current of family life which Elizabeth has come to see through Darcy's eyes. There is a lack of balance in the lives of the younger members of the family: Lydia and Kitty are wholly absorbed in pursuing young men; Mary pores over her books. They live from a purely subjective point of view, unaware of how they may appear to others. Lydia delights in her inconsistency: she is heartless, self-absorbed, interested only in the 'histories of their parties and good jokes' (Chapter 39). Mr Bennet may deplore the behaviour of his youngest daughters, but he cannot influence it.

The second volume of the novel ends with a lull in the action. Lydia accepts an invitation to Brighton, leaving Kitty jealous and despondent. Lydia, looking at her life with the creative eyes of fancy, can see only the glamour of the military at Brighton, while Mr Bennet cannot take seriously the danger Lydia's conduct might do the family. Elizabeth meets Wickham for the last time, and the novel now moves toward a resolution of the conflicts which have been set up by the action so far. In a sense, we may think, the climax of the novel has already taken place: Elizabeth's perception of the world — and of Darcy, in particular — has been reorganised, but there is no obvious way to their reconciliation. *Pride and Prejudice* contains a complicated set of narratives — Lydia's is just about to begin — and Jane Austen's task is to find some way of bringing these loosely-related stories to a coherent conclusion.

## Volume Three (*Chapters 43–61*)

Elizabeth's holiday trip with her aunt and uncle takes her to Derbyshire (not the Lake District) and they visit Pemberley. It is impressive enough to make Elizabeth feel that 'to be mistress of Pemberley might be something.' Now Elizabeth hears a different account of Darcy's character: the housekeeper, who has known him since he was a child, tells her of his sweetness of temper, his attention to his sister, his thoughtfulness to servants. As she looks at a portrait of him she sees him as gentler than she had imagined; now he is the master of an imposing estate, surrounded by servants who speak well of him, and she encounters his pictured glance 'with a deeper sentiment of gratitude than it had ever raised before.' (Portraits, we may note, whether real or imaginary, are significant aids to understanding character in this novel.) Outside she is startled by the appearance of Darcy himself. A second encounter leads to her introducing her aunt and uncle to him, pleased that there are members of her family of whom she feels no shame. Jane Austen's account of the reconciliation is leisurely and serene. Mr and Mrs Gardiner see nothing of the arrogance Elizabeth has attributed to him; his sister, Georgiana, is shy rather than proud. Elizabeth does not confide in her aunt, though Darcy's interest in her is obvious. Jane Austen catches the sense of restraint on either side, the recognition that the relationship is on a new footing, though neither can be sure whether it has ended or is about to develop.

In these chapters at Lambton Mr and Mrs Gardiner act almost as substitute parents for Elizabeth: they are intelligent, respectable, interested and discreet. They reassess Darcy's reputation in the light of their observations and of the reports of him in the village. They deem his pride to be an effect of his social remoteness; they learn he is 'a liberal man' who 'did much good among the poor' (Chapter 44). But Wickham's local reputation is of someone who has left bad debts. Elizabeth is now able to review her own feelings: hate gives way to a respect warmed by the testimony of others and his own altered demeanour. Above all she is grateful to him for ignoring her acrimonious rejection of him. Having re-introduced her to Darcy, Jane Austen now attempts to re-integrate Elizabeth into his social circle. While the gentlemen are out fishing, Elizabeth and Mrs Gardiner pay a rather stiff morning call on the ladies of Pemberley, now augmented by Miss Bingley and Mrs Hurst. On each side there is awkwardness and a formality relaxed only by the appearance of food, 'for though they could not all talk, they could all eat' (Chapter 45). When the gentlemen arrive, Miss Bingley is moved to a malice which Darcy repudiates. Her sneering attacks on Elizabeth rebound on herself and she presents too easy a target for Darcy's crushing rejoinders.

After the slow pace of the opening chapters of the third volume, appropriate to the regeneration of esteem which takes place in them, events move more rapidly when Jane writes to report Lydia's elopement with Wickham. Jane's letter has all the marks of anxious haste; her effort to appear calm breaks down in a frantic appeal for Elizabeth's return. Elizabeth mistakes Darcy's reaction to this news, believing once again that she has lost his good opinion. As she sees him pacing the room in gloomy distraction, she concludes:

> Her power was sinking; everything *must* sink under such a proof of family weakness, such an assurance of the deepest disgrace. She could neither wonder nor condemn, but the belief of his self-conquest brought nothing consolatory to her bosom, afforded no palliation of her distress.
> (*Chapter 46*)

Elizabeth's conclusion that Darcy's self-esteem has sought to defend itself by extinguishing his love for her is not unreasonable in view of her previous knowledge of him, but it ignores what she has recently been told of his generosity and kindness. Jane Austen is careful not to reveal Darcy's attitude to the cause of Elizabeth's distress. His voice, when he speaks to her, 'though it spoke compassion, spoke likewise restraint' (Chapter 46), and it is not clear to Elizabeth whether his assumption that she will not visit Pemberley that afternoon indicates his pity for her or his wish to protect his sister.

The elopement of Lydia and Wickham exposes the weaknesses of the Bennet family. On her return home, Elizabeth finds it difficult to bear Mary's sententiousness; Mrs Bennet's hysterical fantasies prevent her from taking effective action; Jane's benevolence has met with an instance of real evil, and Elizabeth bitterly reproaches herself for not revealing what Darcy had told her about Wickham's character. The Gardiners display a rational firmness of purpose beyond any member of the Bennet family; the problem seems more likely to be solved by their uncle than by their father. Lydia's letter to Colonel Forster's wife displays the levity we would expect from her, but Jane Austen is careful to make it clear that, whatever Wickham's intentions may have been, Lydia meant to marry him.

Now all Meryton agrees that Wickham has been a rascal. He has left nothing behind him but debts; his whereabouts is unknown. At home the family wait anxiously for news, but only Mr Collins sends them a characteristically self-righteous letter, which mixes pity with malice and self-congratulation. When Mr Bennet returns from London where he has searched fruitlessly for his daughter, he has lost none of his wry, but pitiable, cynicism. The sharpness of his wit is merely an index of the weakness of his character. Able to take nothing seriously, he is perpetually at the mercy of events. His levity is no less evident when Mr Gardiner, who has seen the runaways in London, sends a business-like note to set out the terms on which Wickham will marry Lydia. He remains perversely aggrieved that Wickham should marry her for such a petty sum. Jane's prediction that all will now be well is more prescient than Elizabeth's pessimism. She has not taken sufficient account of the fact that shallow natures feel little remorse.

After his exertions in London, Mr Bennet is happy to revert to indolence and leave the management of affairs to Mr Gardiner. Only on one point is he adamant: he will not receive Lydia into his house. Mrs Bennet has no such feelings; she is too excited at the idea of a wedding to think of blaming Lydia. Now that a marriage has been arranged, Elizabeth wishes she had not told Darcy about the elopement. The poignant sense of loss which she had earlier felt is replaced now by more turbulent, restless feelings, in which fantasies about what she supposes Darcy must be feeling veil any clearer vision of him:

> What a triumph for him, as she often thought, could he know that the proposals which she had proudly spurned only four months ago, would now have been gladly and gratefully received. He was as generous, she doubted not, as the most generous of his sex. But while he was mortal, there must be a triumph. (*Chapter 50*)

The word 'triumph' suggests a wealth of pessimistic connotations which cluster round human relationships and sexual relationships in particular. They are a matter of warfare, of victory and defeat, of mastery and enslavement. The word suggests all the rapturous delight of a conqueror gloating over his prisoner. Elizabeth's pessimism is deepened by her sense of the ironic contrast between the ideal partnership which is slipping out of her grasp and the marriage of passion and expediency which is about to be celebrated. Despite Mr Bennet's objections, the bride and bridegroom visit Longbourn, showing none of the feelings judged proper for them. Lydia continues to value her experience according to the 'fun' it has given her. She proudly assumes the position of the married woman and speaks of Wickham with an exuberant lack of tact.

A persistent feature of Jane Austen's narrative technique is the creation of mysteries which require explanation. Letters play a significant part in clearing up what is mysterious in her novels. In *Pride and Prejudice* a sequence of letters from Darcy (in Chapter 35), from Lydia (in Chapter 47) from Mr Collins (in Chapter 48) and from Mr Gardiner (in Chapter 49) has helped to clarify aspects of the novel which Jane Austen has concealed from the reader. Now, Mrs Gardiner's letter (in Chapter 52) explains how Wickham and Lydia were discovered in London by Darcy. He had believed he had not done enough to make Wickham's character generally known. A sense of personal responsibility had led him to pay Wickham's debts, buy him a commission and settle a sum of money on Lydia. In fact, the conceal- ment of the truth about Wickham is the fault of Elizabeth. Darcy has taken the blame for her omission and paid the reparations which she owed. Her aunt's letter is the first sign for Elizabeth that Darcy has not give her up. But she still cannot quite believe it.

The extended report of Elizabeth's reception of her aunt's letter marks another stage in the process of her self-abasement. Now she is full of remorse for her ill-considered mistrust of Darcy. She also discovers a kind of pride — pride in the achievement of another — which need not be damaging:

> For herself she was humbled; but she was proud of him. Proud that in a cause of compassion and honour, he had been able to get the better of himself. (*Chapter 52*)

In perceiving that Darcy has been able to accomplish this new act of self- mastery (he has mastered the self-esteem which has mastered his passion for her), Elizabeth shows that she has established a command over herself. For him she is willing to sacrifice her wit, her sharp observation, her amusement at the expense of others. She is even glad at the pain she feels in Mrs Gardiner's reference to her intimacy with Darcy. Every benefit she might have gained from that relationship is worth losing, if only she knows his value.

An immediate trial of her self-command is provided by Wickham with whom she is able to talk civilly but truthfully. She makes it clear there will be no recriminations about the past, and her hopes for a peaceful future cause him a moment of shame. The departure of Lydia and Wickham is rapidly followed by news of Bingley's return to Netherfield. Soon Bingley and Darcy are riding up to the door at Longbourn. The capitulation of Bingley is reported with a fine grasp of the value of non-verbal signals: he hesitates at his accustomed place beside Jane at table; Mrs Bennet makes no suggestion; Jane turns and smiles, and he sits beside her. Although the for- malities of their engagement take longer, some natural affinity between them finally takes effect.

Elizabeth's reconciliation with Darcy takes longer: they are not placed together; their conversations are interrupted. As a final obstacle in their path, Jane Austen produces Lady Catherine de Bourgh, whose plan to marry Darcy to her daughter has always seemed one of the less likely endings of the novel. The encounter between Lady Catherine and Elizabeth is scarcely cast in the mode of realism. Like Mr Collins, Lady Catherine belongs rather to melodrama or fairy-tale. Although she speaks in the name of reason, she is the personification of family pride and social prejudice, uniting all the defects shown hitherto by Elizabeth and Darcy themselves. Their debate is a re-enactment of the nursery-tale battle of Jack and the Giant. Sure of her capacity for inspiring terror, Lady Catherine underestimates Elizabeth's capacity for self-defence. In the speech-rhythms of her ladyship we hear, perhaps, Jane Austen's final use of literary parody. Consider Lady Catherine's explanation of the bond which exists between her daughter and Darcy, when she argues:

> 'The engagement between them is of a peculiar kind. From their infancy, they have been intended for each other. It was the favourite wish of *his* mother, as well as of hers. While in their cradles, we planned the union: and now, at the moment when the wishes of both sisters would be accomplished, in their marriage, to be prevented by a young woman of inferior birth, of no importance in the world, and wholly unallied to the family! Do you pay no regard to the wishes of his friends? To his tacit engagement with Miss De Bourgh? Are you lost to every feeling of propriety and delicacy? Have you not heard me say that from his earliest hours he was destined for his cousin? (*Chapter 56*)

Lady Catherine's sentences are not meant to inform but to paralyse her opponent. As she moves from statement, to exclamation, to rhetorical question, it is clear that they are no more than an emphatic assertion of her sense of personal authority. Perhaps she does not realise how much she concedes, when she describes the engagement between Darcy and her daughter as 'peculiar'. Elizabeth points out that engagements made between infants can only be ratified if they consent as adults. Lady Catherine's statements, even if they are true, are not attached to any present fact or intention. Elizabeth cannot judge her own position in the world as determined solely by her relationship to Lady Catherine's family. That her ladyship has come to Longbourn gives colour to the rumours of a marriage between Darcy and Elizabeth. Elizabeth refuses to discuss the matter, and although she does tell Lady Catherine truthfully that they are not engaged, she makes no promise not to become so. To the melodramatic rhetoric of Lady Catherine ('Are the shades of Pemberley to be thus polluted?') Elizabeth opposes logic and reason. She does not admit she is Darcy's inferior in social position; she claims the right to act freely according to her own judgment and suggests Darcy is equally free. She makes it plain that empty emotional appeals have no effect on her: an appeal to 'the claims of duty, honour and gratitude' is idle, if no such claims exist. Elizabeth owes nothing to Lady Catherine or her family; the question of the marriage is a private affair.

If the humour of this scene is touched with farce, there is a more serious side to it. The flowing rhythms of Lady Catherine's sentences display a simple-minded self-righteousness that must make us laugh. But Elizabeth's cool self-possession advances the cause of reason against unthinking social deference. That rank of itself confers no authority is an idea alien to the English character. In routing Lady Catherine, Elizabeth displays a radicalism we might hesitate to associate with her creator. But Elizabeth cannot be sure that Darcy does not share his aunt's prejudices. She decides that a test of his intentions will be whether or not he keeps his promise to return to Netherfield. She faces his possible defection with fortitude:

> 'If he is satisfied with only regretting me, when he might have obtained my affections and hand, I shall soon cease to regret him at all.' (*Chapter 57*)

Despite Elizabeth's fears, Mr Darcy comes to Longbourn and Jane Austen brings them alone in talk (Chapter 58). To Elizabeth's thanks for his helping Lydia, he insists that he acted only out of thought for her. She forces herself to tell him how her feelings about him have changed. If it is an act of submission on her part, it is received with pleasure and assurances of her importance to him. At first, Jane Austen is content to present their feelings in summary. She leaves us to imagine their words, noting only the change of expression in their faces. On his there is a look of 'heart-felt delight', while she shyly avoids his eye. Lady Catherine *has* played a part in their love affair by convincing him that Elizabeth has not put him quite out of her mind. As they look back on his first attempt to propose, each regrets what was then said: she regrets her asperity, he his ungentlemanly remarks about her social inferiority. What he has remembered is the look of disdain with which she refused him. What follows is Darcy's account of the sense of humiliation which Elizabeth's reproof has brought him. As opposed to the dramatic presentation of Elizabeth's own self-reproaches, it occupies little space. But it is heart-felt: the past is not to be forgotten, because painful memories help to remind him of the moral faults he now acknowledges. Jane Austen compels him to confess explicitly that he has been

> '. . . a selfish being all my life, in practice, though not in principle. As a child I was taught what was *right*, but I was not taught to correct my temper. I was given good principles, but left to follow them in pride and conceit. (*Chapter 58*)

This is the testimony of the reformed sinner, who has at last seen the error of his ways. For a moment Mr Darcy is no longer a character but a figure from the literature of redemption and edification. But Jane Austen is too skilful to leave him in this position for long. His account of his management of Bingley's return to Jane shows that he has not lost all confidence in his judgment. Elizabeth does not tease him, but it is clear that his new humility has not removed all his blindness about his own motivation.

Elizabeth does not find it easy to make her new status public: too much dislike has been shown to Darcy to be removed in a moment. Even when the secret is revealed to Jane (Chapter 59), Elizabeth can speak only indirectly of her feelings. We cannot quite believe that her love for him dates from 'her first seeing his beautiful grounds at Pemberley', though, of course, Pemberley is not just a place, or a possession, but a social station with manifold responsibilities and opportunities for action. With the example of Charlotte Lucas before her, Elizabeth does not need Jane's advice to 'do anything rather than marry without affection.' Only the reader knows the whole story of the alterations in Elizabeth's feelings for Darcy. Mr Bennet's real affection for his daughter enables him to see her as more than a source of amusement; his concern for her welfare is real and his fear that she would be unhappy with a man she could not respect shows he values her intelligence and respects her integrity. There is no assumption of equality, however, in the marriage: the demands of Elizabeth's intelligence will be satisfied, if she can see that her husband is her superior. For Mrs Bennet, Darcy's wealth is a sufficient guarantee of happiness. In Elizabeth's eyes, Darcy is to be a source of stability and security; her own role is to question and subvert. But each of these roles is to be played within the limits of reason.

The final stages of *Pride and Prejudice* are very considerably condensed, but Jane Austen takes care to ensure that her account of the change in Darcy's mind about Elizabeth, which leads him to change the advice he has given Bingley about Jane, is given substance. It is true that we may not believe that Bingley is much to be admired. As a lover, he is too easily persuaded by the opinions of his friend. But his behaviour before he proposes to Jane is accounted for by the fact that, as Elizabeth puts it, he has waited for his friend's permission. In the same way, Darcy's preoccupied behaviour on his visits to Longbourn is explained by his wish to make fresh observations on the state of Jane's affections. He is, of course, ready to accept that his real motive for going there was to see Elizabeth. Jane Austen has committed herself to linking those two love affairs in a complex way, but she has made every effort to ensure that what she says is internally consistent, so that Bingley's strange neglect of Jane may be accounted for. It is, of course, possible to argue that her explanation of Bingley's apparent lack of interest is simply a rationalisation of her need to keep Jane and Bingley apart while she manages the difficult task of finding ways of bringing Elizabeth and Darcy together: the psychological implausibility of one of these relationships could then be seen as a measure of the immaturity of her technical skill.

Another answer to the puzzle about Darcy and Bingley's relationship is that Bingley has accepted Darcy as a model of social behaviour, since Bingley's own social standing is less well-established. But the events of the novel have forced Darcy to revise his claim to set such a standard. In giving Bingley 'permission' to declare his love for Jane, he is surely acknowledging the claims of spontaneous natural affection and of that open, loving spirit which Jane Austen calls 'candour', and which Jane Bennet displays throughout the novel. But Jane Austen sets a limit to the concessions to human nature which she demands of Darcy: he is allowed to keep his pride, to the extent that it reflects a proper concern for human values. The course of the novel may have compelled him to revise what these standards are, but no concession is made to vulgarity or obsequiousness or insincerity. There will be no place at Pemberley for the meanness and falsity so often shown at Longbourn, Meryton and Netherfield.

# Chapter 5

# Mansfield Park:
## judging others

## Introduction

A summary of the 'events' of *Mansfield Park* makes the novel sound thin: five children—the Bertrams and Fanny Price—grow up into young people who fall in love and think about marriage. A heavy, distant, scarcely agreeable father orders their lives, abruptly forbids their interest in play-acting and knows little about their inner lives. He does not understand the niece whom he has brought up, just failing to force her to marry a man she does not love. Of the other, older, people in the novel, Lady Bertram is weak and silly; Mrs Norris, her sister, is selfish, snobbish and spiteful. The central character, Fanny Price, is—it may be thought—too good to be true. What can be said in the novel's defence?

*Mansfield Park* focuses on a small number of families in the kind of community Jane Austen knew best. Fanny Price and the Bertrams form a closely knit, yet diverse, group of people whose principal contact outside the family circle is with the clergyman at the parsonage, Dr Grant, a lazy, worldly clergyman, whose company is rendered tolerable by his livelier wife. In terms of *Pride and Prejudice*, it is as if we were situated at Rosings or Pemberley rather than at Longbourn. Through Mrs Grant, the Bertrams are introduced to Mary and Henry Crawford. Together with the Rushworths of Sotherton Court, whose owner Maria Bertram marries, they almost complete the principal figures in the narrative. Mention is occasionally made of the family servants or acquaintances used to illustrate a point in conversation, but secondary figures are not relied on (as they are in *Pride and Prejudice*) as necessary links in the action. Within the orbit of Mansfield itself are concentrated all the diverse types of character which are more freely distributed in the earlier novel. Separate from, and in contrast to, the splendour of Mansfield Park is the restrictiveness of the Price household in Portsmouth, which suggests the limitations of poverty and the penalties of disorder. Portsmouth, London and Mansfield are invested with a symbolic force which produces a strong but perhaps rather schematic effect.

If some of these contrasts appear in the earlier novels, *Mansfield Park* is richer and deeper for at least three reasons: it is organised with much greater care; it examines in greater depth the values it recommends; and it produces a conflict between opposing forces of good and evil which is more subtly rendered than any such conflict in Jane Austen's earlier fiction. There is greater control over the design of the novel: episodes are now grouped to form sequences of action, small in themselves, which are given significance by their place in the structure as a whole. As in her previous novels, conversation forms a significant part of the action. Jane Austen's capacity for inducing characters to reveal themselves unwittingly in speech has been developed to a higher power. But despite evident gains in technical resourcefulness, it may be argued that some essential quality of her character as a writer has been held in check in this deeply serious novel. In *Mansfield Park* she betrays greatest unease about the value of 'wit'.

# Commentary

## Volume One (*Chapters 1–18*)

Perhaps the first thing to notice about *Mansfield Park* is the rapidity with which Jane Austen assembles the circle of characters who are to form the basis of the action. In Chapter 1 Fanny Price, the little girl who is to be assimilated into the Bertram family, is nine years old; by Chapter 3, she is fifteen. Jane Austen retains our belief by including enough detail to suggest the passage of time. At the beginning of Chapter 2, for example, we find that Fanny is in fact ten years old, and in that second chapter her relations with the children of the house are quickly established. Responsibility for establishing our sense of the essential features of the situation of the newcomer rests with the narrative voice of the novel, as may be seen in the account of Fanny's welcome from the Bertram girls ('The holiday allowed to the Miss Bertrams the next day . . . or wasting gold paper.' (Chapter 2)). The special skill of this writing is both to enter into, and to remain outside, the feelings and attitudes of the characters whose behaviour is being described. The narrator enters into the feelings of the Misses Bertram but does not sympathise with what she finds there. The observation 'They could not but hold her cheap' not only says something about what Maria and Julia value, it tells us something about how they arrive at their judgments. All that matters to them are their cousin's possessions: if her rating on this scale is low, they feel compelled to scorn her. In the same way, they feel obliged to give her a gift which will not only show how little they value her, but will require her to be grateful to them. The sisters' selfishness and superficiality, and their complacent expectation of being admired, are implied by the tone of the paragraph. They value items of knowledge as a kind of possession, whereas the narrator obviously believes that 'self-knowledge, generosity and humility' (Chapter 2) are more valuable than well-stocked memories.

Their aunt and their father share some of the blame for their failings: Mrs Norris reinforces their groundless sense of superiority, while Sir Thomas Bertram is too distant to know them as they really are. Not for the first time are we reminded of the dangers of parental shortcomings. Sir Thomas's reserve is matched by Lady Bertram's indolence. Together, the responsible adults of Mansfield Park make an unsatisfactory trio: a withdrawn father, a dull and negligent mother, an interfering aunt, who is ignorant, intemperate and partial. Only Edmund, the younger son, has shown the little girl kindness—the supreme kindness of helping Fanny to write to her own much-loved brother, William. That relationship provides an instance of Jane Austen's apparent belief that the affection between brother and sister can provide a foundation for the future bond between husband and wife. In this new family, Edmund treats Fanny like a considerate brother. Unlike that of Maria and Julia, his behaviour has no reference to himself. He is truly generous, thinking only of what will support and sustain Fanny, encouraging her 'fondness of reading, which, properly directed, must be an education in itself' (Chapter 2).

The pace of the novel (which has brought Fanny to the edge of maturity) slackens slightly with the departure of Sir Thomas and his eldest son to the West Indies, but only to introduce us more fully to the characters who are left behind. Now we are aware of the succession of seasons rather than of years. Departing in the Spring, the travellers are expected back in September, though only Tom returns then. Maria and Julia have been launched in local society; Fanny remains at home as Lady Bertram's companion. Edmund buys a horse so that Fanny can ride it; Mr John Rushworth proposes to Maria; and Mr and Miss Crawford arrive to visit their half-sister, Mrs Grant. It is the following July; Fanny is eighteen. The principal characters are assembled; the compression of time into four chapters of narrative can now give place to the more measured pace of dramatised action.

The arrival of the Crawfords saves Mrs Grant from domestic boredom. Mary Crawford has left the household to which her guardian uncle, Admiral Crawford, had brought his mistress; Henry Crawford has a horror of settling down. In their first conversation, Mrs Grant sketches a possible future for them: Mary will marry Tom Bertram, because he is Sir Thomas's heir; Henry will flirt with Tom's sisters, but avoid marriage, since, according to Mary, 'the admiral's lessons have quite spoiled him' (Chapter 4). It is, of course, common knowledge that Maria is engaged. The conversation is high-spirited and spoken for effect. It will be for the action of the novel to determine how seriously we are meant to take it.

Maria and Julia Bertram feel obliged to marry men who can give them what they want. John Rushworth could give Maria (Chapter 4) 'the enjoyment of a larger income than her father's, as well as ensure the house in town, which was now a prime object', so it was 'her evident duty to marry Mr Rushworth if she could.' Similarly, 'Miss Bertram's engagement made

[Henry Crawford] in equity the property of Julia' (Chapter 5). We have already noticed this narrative voice, adept at preserving in objective prose questionable opinions which it records without comment. Although no moral comment is made by the narrator, Maria's mercenary attitudes, her self-interest and her capacity for self-deception are made plain. Julia's assumption that Henry should be her 'property' matches Maria's attitude to John Rushworth: that Henry should be hers 'in equity' implies that the sisters expect the good things of the world to be divided between them, and that if no law provides for this, natural justice should ensure a proper distribution. Unfortunately, Henry Crawford finds he is attracted to Maria. Mary Crawford is cynical about marriage; for her, it is 'a manoeuvring business', a matter of mutual manipulation — 'of all transactions, [it is] the one in which people expect most from others, and are least honest themselves' (Chapter 5). Mary uses a form of language appropriate to the expression of a universal truth, but the author implicitly challenges the reader to accept or reject the offered statement. Indeed, the action of the novel will provide a test of her statement's truth.

Now that the characters are assembled, Jane Austen sets them in motion. Tom Bertram is perhaps the most disposable of them, his main function being to offer a contrast to the virtues of his brother, Edmund, and perhaps to cast doubts on the advantages of primogeniture. Having returned home long enough to attract Mary Crawford's attention, he is removed to pursue his sporting interests, and to leave the way clear for the first of Jane Austen's enquiries into the nature of love. There is now no clumsiness about her management of the three groups of lovers — Mary, Edmund and Fanny; Julia, Henry and Maria; and Maria, Henry and John Rushworth. Their relationships are explored during a visit to Mr Rushworth's property at Sotherton, which has been arranged so that Henry can advise him how to improve it. In the absence of Tom Bertram, Mary's attention has begun to focus on Edmund. He, for his part, has not found her liveliness wholly appealing. He has, however, allowed her

> . . . the right of a lively mind . . . seizing whatever may contribute to its own amusement or that of others; perfectly allowable, when untinctured by ill-humour or roughness . . . (*Chapter 7*)

We are expected to grant the reasonableness of this view, and even to feel that Fanny must be wrong. It is another instance of Jane Austen's difficulty in deciding what principles should guide the use of a sharp and witty tongue.

Edmund is sure that Mary is neither ill-humoured or rough; in fact he is in love with her. Mary responds to his interest, though the narrator suggests she cannot understand it:

> . . . [Edmund] was not pleasant by any common rule, he talked no nonsense, he paid no compliments, his opinions were unbending, his attentions tranquil and simple. There was a charm, perhaps, in his sincerity,

his steadiness, his integrity, which Miss Crawford might be equal to feel, though not equal to discuss with herself. (*Chapter 7*)

Here, it is 'the common rule' of judgment which is placed under the narrator's ironic regard: Edmund's does not measure up to the usual requirements for conventional approval. Mary may be able to feel the force of his character even if she cannot analyse it; she does not know what she admires. It is also a transient feeling which she is content to entertain while he is near her.

Fanny does not quite agree with Edmund about Mary; she learns to bear his absences, however, and is caused pain only when he begins to teach Mary to ride on the horse he had bought for Fanny's use. We follow with sympathy Fanny's awkward feelings — her faint resentment, her wish not to believe her relationship with Edmund has changed, her feelings of rejection, her painful sense of a duty to suppress her own feelings for the sake of others. These disagreeable emotions — strong enough to produce a headache — are not allayed by Mrs Norris's unjust accusations of laziness. Lady Bertram's ingenuous recital of what she thinks has produced Fanny's headache reveals how ill-natured Mrs Norris's description has been. Edmund blames himself for what has happened:

His own forgetfulness of her was worse than anything which they [her aunts] had done. Nothing of this would have happened had she been properly considered; but she had been left four days together without any choice of companions, and without any excuse for avoiding whatever her unreasonable aunts might require. (*Chapter 7*)

It is a good example of the reflectiveness which is beyond the reach of Mary Crawford.

A similar application of intelligence improves Fanny's chances of visiting Sotherton. Edmund offers to act as Lady Bertram's companion, until Mrs Grant volunteers to stay behind, thus freeing Edmund to be with Mary. Now Mrs Grant adroitly secures for Julia the seat on the carriage beside Henry. As Fanny and Mary gaze back at Edmund, who is on horseback behind them, the contrast between them is pressed home:

. . . in every thing but a value for Edmund, Miss Crawford was very unlike her. She had none of Fanny's delicacy of taste, of mind, of feeling; she saw nature, inanimate nature with little observation; her attention was all for men and women, her talents for the light and lively. (*Chapter 8*)

This comparison of Fanny and Mary gives place to a more extended deployment of groups of three (Chapter 9): Henry Crawford, John Rushworth and Maria are linked by their interest in the 'improvement' of Sotherton. Edmund, Mary and Fanny 'seemed as naturally to unite'; and Mrs Rushworth, Mrs Norris and Julia — to Julia's discomfiture — make up the remainder. Julia restrains her feelings, but by rule, rather than by a self-disciplined sense of correct behaviour.

Jane Austen leaves Julia's jealous fretfulness and returns to Edmund's group as they explore the grounds of Sotherton. The grounds are carefully described: the lawn leads to a terrace walk overlooking a 'wilderness', which is nevertheless 'laid out with too much regularity'; access to it is by an unlocked door; a straight avenue leads to a locked iron gate through which the park can be seen. Beside this gate, overlooking the park, is a comfortable bench. At first, Edmund, Mary and Fanny wander among the shade of the trees. Mary Crawford takes up the question of Edmund's future profession. No one would choose to become a clergyman voluntarily, since it confers no distinction. As she puts it, 'A clergyman is nothing.' Edmund's reply is deliberate and weighty; in his eyes, clergymen are, or ought to be, patterns of conduct to their parishioners:

'. . . it will, I believe, be every where found, that as the clergy are, or are not what they ought to be, so are the rest of the nation.' (*Chapter 9*)

If there seems a touch of sententious complacency about Edmund's words, Fanny, nevertheless, agrees 'with gentle earnestness', though Mary is unconvinced. When Fanny feels tired, he offers her his arm, and hopes Mary will take the other one. Mary ascribes Fanny's tiredness to the boredom of looking at great houses, and finds no refreshment, as Fanny does, in looking out at the greenness of the park beyond.

Fanny is now left sitting on the bench as a lonely spectator of the behaviour of the remaining groups. Maria, Henry and John arrive, eagerly discussing changes to the property. Finding the park-gate locked, they send John off for the key. Left alone with Maria (Fanny's presence makes no difference), Henry addresses her in the intimate tone he used earlier in the chapel when he expressed a wistful regret at her approaching marriage. Though she re-directs his attention to Julia, Maria is not sorry to find that the comparison between them leads to compliments in her favour. Married to Mr Rushworth, she implies, she will be a bird in a gilded cage. Her apprehension about the kind of marriage John can offer her becomes linked with her impatient wait for the key. Henry's comment acts as a challenge:

'And for the world you would not get out without the key and without Mr Rushworth's authority and protection, or I think you might with a little difficulty pass round the edge of the gate, here, with my assistance; I think it might be done, if you really wished to be more at large, and could allow yourself to think it not prohibited.' (*Chapter 10*)

It is the final word which Maria seizes upon to answer, 'Prohibited! nonsense! I can certainly get out that way, and I will.'

It is obvious that her wilfulness is her unthinking response to Henry's seductive suggestion, but her unrestrained behaviour in this minor matter foreshadows a susceptibility to temptation of a more serious kind. Now, the stretch of ground between Fanny's bench and the iron gates of the park becomes a kind of stage which Fanny overlooks as a spectator, while the reader watches from a more distant point of view. Julia, glad to escape from Mrs Rushworth, enters in pursuit of Henry and takes her sister's route into the park. Tired of waiting, Fanny goes to look for companions, only to find them returning from inspecting the avenue of trees which is destined to be cut down and which she had longed to see.

Jane Austen manages these scenes with finely judged dramatic skill. The comings and goings of her characters are far from being merely farcical. Each stage of the action pulls tighter the knot she is creating for them: more heartache is provided for Fanny, more discomfiture for John Rushworth, more exposure to moral danger for Maria and Julia. Fanny and her companions now rejoin the older ladies to wait for Maria, Julia, Henry and John to return from the park. They ought to be suitably paired off, but only Maria and Henry are happy. The complex scene Jane Austen has created is reduced to the myopic complacency of Mrs Norris's, 'Well, Fanny, this has been a fine day for you, upon my word! . . . Nothing but pleasure from beginning to end.'

The prospect of Sir Thomas's return generates a chapter of conversation (Chapter 11) which explores the relationship between Fanny and Edmund and Mary Crawford. Mary complains that Edmund and Maria are to be sacrificed, as she puts it, to Sir Thomas's parental aspirations — Edmund as a clergyman, Maria as a bride. In Mary's view, Edmund has chosen to be a clergymen because his father is able to provide him with a living — that is, a clergyman's job to which he can appoint whom he pleases. Edmund accepts that the living played a part in his decision, but denies that all clergymen are selfish and indolent, as she describes them. As he puts it,

'Where any one body of educated men, of whatever denomination, are condemned indiscriminately, there must be a deficiency of information, or (smiling) of something else.' (*Chapter 11*)

The 'something else' is not specified, but the precautionary smile before the phrase suggests there might be some offence if Edmund were more precise: it is left to Mary to surmise whether she would be thought wanting in good sense or good nature. When she offers Dr Grant as an example of what she means, Fanny defends him: he must do less harm as a clergyman than as anything else, and in his profession he is compelled to think. Edmund's word of praise for Fanny sends her in embarrassment to the window (a characteristic place of refuge for Jane Austen's less assertive heroines), and Mary (perhaps in some pique) joins the others. As Edmund joins her, Fanny once more displays her deep feeling of pleasure in Nature, which she has no difficulty in putting into words. She is not only able to enjoy what she sees; she can give a reason for the special moral value of contemplating the natural world. It helps to free the self—of meditation and reflection—from the selfish preoccupations that beset the natural man or woman.

The final stage of the first volume ends with the amateur theatricals which cause such dismay. The choice of play—*Lovers' Vows*, by the German dramatist Kotzebue (1761–1819)—throws some light on Fanny's objections. Its story is that Agatha, who has been seduced and abandoned many years before by Baron Wildenhaim, is found in poverty by Frederick, her grown-up son, who has been sent home from the army to fetch his birth-certificate. She has to tell him he is illegitimate. While begging for money for his mother, he threatens two rich gentlemen, one or whom turns out to be his father. The other is the rather foppish suitor of the Baron's daughter, Amelia, who is obediently entering into marriage with a man she does not love to please her father's desire for wealth. In fact, she is in love with her father's chaplain, Anhalt, to whom she declares her love. Her father rejects her rich suitor, Count Cassel, when his rakish past is revealed, while the revelation of his own betrayal of Agatha brings about their reconciliation and marriage. The unsuitability of the play lies less in its indelicacy than in its closeness to the situation at Mansfield Park. The relationship between Amelia and Count Cassel resembles that between Maria and John Rushworth; Edmund is preparing to be a clergyman, and he has formed the mind and character of Fanny Price, who is secretly in love with him. If Mary Crawford plays the part of Amelia, she will be able to declare her love for Edmund on stage. Like Fanny, Agatha had been taken into the household of a wealthy family. That Agatha should then have been seduced by one of the sons suggests the unpleasant possibilities which might befall a girl in such an exposed position. Jane Austen does not make all of these parallels explicit but they may well suggest that *Lovers' Vows* was not a suitable choice of play for an amateur group who, not being accustomed to what Edmund calls 'hardened real acting' (Chapter 13), might find it difficult to separate art from life.

The allocation of the parts in the play stirs up jealousy between Maria and Julia, who both want to play Agatha to the Frederick of Henry Crawford. Henry inflames the jealousy by suggesting that he could not take Julia seriously as his afflicted mother. Edmund hopes Maria will support his disapproval of the play by refusing the part. But Julia would take the part if she refused it. Mrs Norris supports Maria's views that their plan cannot now be altered. Mary Crawford takes the matter as settled, though it is clear from her 'glancing half fearfully, half slily, beyond Fanny to Edmund' (Chapter 15), that she knows of his opposition. When Fanny tries to resist taking even the smallest part, she receives a characteristic reproof from Mrs Norris who reproves her for her obstinacy and ingratitude, and reminds her of her very humble position in the household.

After this episode, for the first time Jane Austen takes us into Fanny's confidence. We follow her to the old school-room which she has been allowed to make her own. She has come a long way from the girl who (in Chapter 2) 'crept about in constant terror of something or other; often retreating towards her own chamber to cry', but she still suffers the ill-nature and disdain of some of her relatives. What she has done is to establish a space for herself, where she can keep her treasures and escape from the pressures to conform to the standards of her female cousins and her aunts. Here she can 'muse' — not day-dream, but think. On this occasion her concern is whether she is right to disoblige her cousins by refusing a part in the play. Jane Austen dramatises the difficulty of settling a complex moral issue. Fanny mainly relies on Edmund's judgment that his father would disapprove of what was being done. But that resource fails her when Edmund himself asks her advice about whether he should take a part which would otherwise be taken by someone outside their group. What principally concerns him is what Miss Crawford feels about it, and he argues that only by participating himself can he limit the danger the play might cause. Fanny's thoughts, when he leaves her, are desolate: Edmund has retreated from his principles; he has mainly been swayed by Mary's influence and perhaps by unexpected feelings of jealousy that some unknown young man will play opposite her. He agrees that the others will 'triumph' over him, but loss of Mary's goodwill is more important than the defeat of a principle. Jane Austen is careful to make the point that Tom and Maria are well aware of why Edmund has capitulated: he has come off his moral high horse; he is no better than they are, after all.

As the preparations for the play become more urgent, Fanny becomes a spectator. But she finds she can enjoy the performances. Little as she likes Henry Crawford as a man, she can admire his acting. What she dreads most is to witness the third act of the play where Amelia, the character played by Mary Crawford, expresses her feelings of love for Anhalt, played by Edmund. Both, in turn, come to Fanny's room to ask her to hear their lines. We are taken into Fanny's consciousness as she prompts them ('She was invested, indeed, with the office of judge and critic . . . she deserved their pity more than she hoped they would ever surmise!' (Chapter 18)). She does not shrink from acknowledging her own feelings of depression ('She felt herself becoming too nearly nothing to both, to have any comfort in having been sought by either'), but she manages, with some difficulty, to dissociate her judgment of their performance from the feelings it arouses in her. She refuses to approve of what they are doing, but she can see they are doing it well. To offer an evaluation of their performance would be to give it tacit approval; to offer criticisms of it might mean running the risk of exposing the feelings of disapproval and of jealousy which the project rouses in her. But Fanny is firm enough to deal with her suffering in private; it is not projected as envy or hatred or revenge. In contrast to Maria and Julia, she tries to regulate her behaviour by reference to a principle, and to be faithful to it whatever happens. Even Fanny's resolve is to be tested to its limit. When Dr Grant falls ill, she is asked to read Mrs Grant's part and, despite her aversion to the play, she gives in. She is saved only by the unexpected arrival of Sir Thomas.

The climax has been carefully prepared for, but it takes the actors completely by surprise. What is striking about Jane Austen's management of the narrative is how successful she has been in making these fairly trivial events the vehicle for the extended analysis of the moral dilemmas generated by personal relationships, with all the psychological and emotional knots and tangles usually associated with them. In contrast to her management of the material of *Pride and Prejudice*, the design of the first volume of *Mansfield Park* is lucid, integrated and logical. Jane Austen has constructed a pattern of events among her sets of characters which is dynamic and progressive; we can trace the chain of actions and reactions which have been generated within the company at Mansfield Park. There is a satisfying completeness about Jane Austen's account of it; it is as if we were watching a fully reported physical or chemical process, none of whose effects have gone unnoticed. Central to the action is Fanny Price: despite her isolation and her exposure to unaccustomed and humiliating feelings of jealousy and envy, she has maintained her composure, her self-reliance and integrity. She has adhered to what she thought was right, even when deserted by the only other person whose judgment she respects.

## Volume Two (*Chapters 19–31*)

Sir Thomas's return alters the course of the action. His children join him in the drawing-room with mixed feelings (Chapter 19). Fanny, apprehensive and concerned in particular for Edmund, remains behind with the Crawfords and Tom's friend, Mr Yates. The former know Sir Thomas well enough to understand that the play is at an end. Only Mr Yates is selfish enough to believe that the acting matters more than this long-delayed family reunion. First, we follow Fanny as she leaves 'to perform the dreadful duty of appearing before her uncle.' We hesitate with her at the door of the drawing-room, share her surprise at her uncle's kindness to her and watch his good humour, firm under the officiousness of Mrs Norris, disintegrating in the face of Mr Yates's insensitivity. Jane Austen is especially good at noting the non-verbal signals of disquiet that his behaviour produces as he talks about the play. Only Fanny and Edmund see Sir Thomas's feelings of disappointment that Edmund, whose judgment he trusted, has let him down, so that he feels 'bewildered in his own house' and made 'part of a ridiculous exhibition in the midst of theatrical nonsense.' A mention of the Crawfords leads to Mr Rushworth's confession of his reservations about acting. Sir Thomas is pleased to agree with him: now that he is home, old standards of behaviour have been re-established. It is difficult for the modern reader to understand Sir Thomas's complete lack of sympathy for the amateur theatricals. Perhaps it is enough to say that Sir Thomas is not presented as a wholly admirable figure—an imperfect capacity for sympathy is his major flaw—and yet there is enough that is objectionable about what is happening to justify some of his displeasure.

With the collapse of the play, the party disintegrates. Henry Crawford departs for London, leaving Maria to suffer the pains of desertion. When Yates follows, Mansfield Park settles back into its accustomed routines. Sir Thomas does not bring any renewed clarity of moral vision: Edmund still loves Mary; Maria is content to smother her doubts about her approaching marriage. She has no intention of allowing Mr Crawford to ruin her hopes of material improvement. Despite his misgivings about John Rushworth, Sir Thomas does not persuade Maria to confide in him fully. The liberty her father's absence had given her was now a necessity and she is

> . . . prepared for matrimony by an hatred of home, restraint, and tranquillity; by the misery of disappointed affection, and contempt of the man she was to marry. (*Chapter 21*)

It is in this frame of mind—wonderfully conveyed by Jane Austen's cool, measured prose, which neither spares nor condemns—that Maria marries John Rushworth and departs on a honeymoon with Julia in attendance. The way has been cleared for the next episode in the testing of Fanny Price.

As a result of a chance downpour, Fanny finds herself becoming more intimately acquainted with Mary Crawford. Fanny knows it is 'an intimacy resulting principally from Miss Crawford's desire for something new,' (Chapter 22) and perhaps it is a sign of weakness on Fanny's part that she finds in her visits to Mary 'a kind of fascination'. The association is at the uneasy level of the aimless attachment of lonely people. Mary does not share Fanny's interests, nor does she have her curiosity and breadth of mind. As we learned in the wilderness at Sotherton, she is indifferent to accuracy. Are the clouds threatening—or have they passed over? Mary is indifferent, so long as they keep Fanny with her. When Fanny talks about the power of memory—in terms which recall her talk with Edmund about the beauty of the night sky—Mary 'untouched and inattentive, had nothing to say.' When Fanny talks about the beauty of the shrubbery, Mary can only express her delight at being there. While Fanny takes pleasure in thinking of the heroism she associates with Edmund's name, Mary can admire it only if she imagines it preceded by a title.

When Edmund joins them, Fanny once more finds herself a spectator. General conversation, which Mary contrives to direct towards the state of her own well-being, gives place to a more intimate conversation between Edmund and herself. Mary leaves him in no doubt that she desires wealth;

he makes it equally clear that what he aspires to has something to do with her. Mary's tone towards Edmund is teasing and ironical; she cannot believe that with his social connections he should be satisfied with 'the middle state of worldly circumstances'. She expects her man to be ambitious, and she cannot believe that Edmund would be satisfied with the obscurity of a country parsonage.

The pleasure that Fanny can now take in being sought after socially is tempered by the pain of the ambiguity of her position. She is Lady Bertram's niece—but she is also a poor relation, a fact of which Mrs Norris constantly reminds her. Although Mrs Norris owes her own position to the accident of her sister's marriage, she does not think of herself as having anything in common with Fanny, nor does she take to herself the words she addresses to her niece about

> 'The nonsense and folly of people's stepping out of their rank and trying to appear above themselves . . . ' (*Chapter 23*)

The partiality, opiniativeness and arrogance of these remarks would be insupportable if they did not accuse the speaker of the faults she condemns in Fanny. When Fanny is invited to dinner at Mrs Grant's, Sir Thomas makes it clear he expects Fanny to be treated like any other member of the family. The carriage is ordered for her and, at Mrs Grant's, she is treated as 'the principal lady in company'. But instead of there being five at dinner, she finds that Henry Crawford has returned to make a sixth.

The dinner party demonstrates once more how Jane Austen uses conversation as a kind of action. The ebb and flow of talk has many dimensions: beneath its disciplined public surface lie the currents of private feeling which public events set up in the participants. The absence of Edmund, talking apart with Dr Grant, allows Henry to speak to his sister about Maria and Julia in the less than respectful tones they reserve for absent friends. He remembers with pleasure the play-acting Fanny can think of only with embarrassment. He had never been happier, but she can remember his behaviour only with indignation. When Henry persists in associating Fanny with his own impressions, for a moment her feelings break through the surface, 'and when her speech was over, she trembled and blushed at her own daring' (Chapter 23). If Henry senses her rebuff, his gravity is short-lived. Before long, he is teasing Edmund about the wealth and ease ordination will bring him. Mary cannot conceal her vexation that Edmund has not been affected by the dislike she has expressed for his chosen profession. Henceforth, she treats Edmund's attentions as a matter for amusement only, but it is an amusement she does not intend to forego.

Henry Crawford has also decided to amuse himself: with his decision to remain for another fortnight at Mansfield and to make, as he puts it, 'a small hole in Fanny Price's heart' (Chapter 24), the purpose of the second volume of the novel becomes clear. A new intimacy has been established between brother and sister; we now see more clearly the sinister side of their characters; we overhear conversations where they do not conceal their distrust of serious or generous feeling. Henry has been impressed, as was Sir Thomas, by Fanny's improved looks, but he is piqued that she does not admire him. He wants to seize her attention by some act of male self-assertion. His intentions are entirely selfish: Fanny is an organism which must be attuned and attached to him. When he says, 'I only want her to look kindly on me, to give me smiles as well as blushes', he is sketching a cold-hearted programme of seduction which might succeed. Fanny is impressionable: were her affections not already firmly fixed on Edmund, Henry Crawford might well be successful.

But, however representative he might be of male vanity, Henry Crawford is guilty of seeking to arouse feelings he has no intention of satisfying. He uses his knowledge of Fanny's affection for her brother, William, to ingratiate himself. William's arrival allows us to see the genuine unaffected feelings which he and Fanny share. As so often in the novels, the feelings between brother and sister establish a standard of affection against which all other kinds of love are measured. In contrast with Henry's sketch of how he might relate to her, the keynote of this friendship is its reciprocity. One of its most significant features is shared memory. Fanny's affection for William is the one incontestable example of human warmth in the novel so far, providing a contrast to the more brittle intimacy of Henry and Mary Crawford, which may be described as complicity rather than love. The Crawford's knowledge of one another is of deviousness and even of evil which they are careful to conceal from others. Of Fanny and William, however, it can be said that 'an affection so amiable was advancing each in the opinion of all who had hearts to value anything good' (Chapter 24).

Out of the changes following Sir Thomas's return home and the departure of Tom and Julia and Maria, a new pattern of social life emerges. Sir Thomas condescends to visit the Grants and begins to notice Henry's interest in Fanny. In talking to her, Henry reverts to the theme of improvement which had prompted their visit to Sotherton. He feels no compunction about remembering that visit and its consequences, but his effrontery makes Fanny blush. When he regrets that Sir Thomas's return had ruined their theatricals, she cannot look at him, and is forced to say:

> 'As far as *I* am concerned, sir, I would not have delayed his return for a day. My uncle disapproved [of] it all so entirely when he did arrive, that in my opinion, everything had gone quite far enough.' (*Chapter 23*)

Fanny is aware that it is her longest speech to him and her angriest to anyone. For a time, his attention is diverted to the parsonage at Thornton Lacey, which had been reserved for Edmund who is soon to become a clergyman. In his mind's eye, Henry sweeps away everything that links the parsonage to the agricultural life around it, transforming it from a clergyman's house to a gentlemen's residence, but when he offers to become the tenant of Thornton Lacey — thus bringing himself closer to Mansfield Park — Sir Thomas makes it clear that only by residing in the living he is to be given can Edmund carry out his clerical duties successfully.

Gradually, it becomes clear that the structure of the second volume of the novel does not have the marshalled brilliance of the first. The action is teased out of the apparently random conversations which take place during routine evening activities at Mansfield Park or at the Grants. Beneath them, Jane Austen traces the changing pattern of relationship which the conversations only half reveal. Henry Crawford's imagined improvements to Thornton Lacey conjure up in Mary's mind agreeable fancies which are shattered by Sir Thomas's solemn words about the duties of a clergyman. To the attentive observer, the history of Fanny's feelings for Henry is related in her looks, her silences and in the attitudes of her body even more clearly than by her words. Decisive differences in attitude to the Church, to the business of making money, to what constitutes an acceptable social ambition and, above all, to the duties of a landowning family towards those for whom it is responsible, are revealed in those conversations. In none of her other novels does Jane Austen lay so much stress on the significance of shared opinion.

Sir Thomas has been sufficiently struck by the image of goodness represented by the mutual love of his nephew and niece to arrange a ball for them. Edmund is pleased at his father's gesture but troubled about his own future. The day after the ball, Edmund is to leave to prepare for ordination, and William is to return to his ship. Edmund's pleasure at his cousin's happiness is real, but detached. He is considering Mary as a wife but cannot clearly see where her affections lie. There is on Edmund's side a limit to his affection for Mary, as well as a blindness about the nature of her 'disinterested attachment' (Chapter 26). His meditations on marriage are coolly rational, although they rest on an idealised view of Mary, not shared by Fanny Price. But he acknowledges that his hopes of her may be defeated by established patterns of interest and habit on either side, which constitute an essential core of self, and which the attraction they feel for one another may not (and, in his case, should not) alter.

Fanny is only concerned to find a way of wearing to the ball the amber cross which William had given her as a present. But this brings her into undesirable intimacy with Henry, since Mary persuades her to accept a necklace which Henry had given her. Cross and necklace are the emblems of a brother's love; what distinguishes them, perhaps, is the quality of the affection which each signifies. Fanny had gone to Mary for advice and chosen the necklace she seemed most willing to give her, only to find it has been forced on her attention to put her under an obligation to Henry. The narrator is careful not to attribute this thought immediately to Fanny. But as a result of Mary's arch remarks, she begins to recognise that Henry's intentions towards her are no different than they had been to Maria and Julia, and suspects that Henry has prompted Mary's offer.

Her confusion is immediately tempered by Edmund's gift of a plain gold chain which will suit the cross far better. But Edmund is anxious not to hurt Mary's feelings (Chapter 27). When he says, 'I would not have the shadow of a coolness arise . . . between the two dearest objects I have on earth', Fanny's feelings for him are painfully precipitated into consciousness:

> She had never heard him speak so openly before, and though it told her no more than what she had long perceived, it was a stab; — for it told of his own convictions and views. They were decided. He would marry Miss Crawford. It was a stab, in spite of every long-standing expectation; and she was obliged to repeat again and again that she was one of his two dearest before the words gave her any sensation. (*Chapter 27*)

The repetitions in these sentences suggest the helplessness of her dismay and disappointment. She has been wounded to the point where feeling is anaesthetised, and she struggles to give herself a firm idea of what she means to Edmund:

> It was her intention, as she felt it to be her duty, to try to overcome all that was excessive, all that bordered on selfishness in her affection for Edmund. To call or to fancy it a loss, a disappointment, would be a presumption; for which she had no words strong enough to satisfy her own humility. To think of him as Miss Crawford might be justified in thinking, would in her be insanity. (*Chapter 27*)

Ordinary people who know how much selfishness and self-deception there can be in the demands which we make on those with whom we are in love will surely acknowedge that Fanny sets herself an almost frightening standard of self-control. It is plain what pressure she is under from the desires she wishes to suppress; she even believes she should be strong enough to prevent the idea of wanting Edmund for herself from entering her mind. If ever Fanny Price appeared lacking in strength of character, it is not now: her absolute commitment to a love which is wholly directed towards the welfare of the loved one and her unwavering dedication to being clear about what that welfare is must surely strike the reader as heroic.

At the ball, Fanny's excitement rises as she begins to realise what it means to be the centre of attention. She is now regarded as a beauty by her uncle and the young men. To her bewilderment, she is being generally admired, and expected to give a lead: she is being treated as one of the family. Even Sir Thomas is 'proud of his niece' (Chapter 28). She endures the formalities which her elders love, but her attention is still on Edmund and Mary Crawford who are clearly in love.

Nothing that happens at the ball clarifies the relationships between the principal characters of the novel, but Mary, affable to everyone else, vexes Edmund by her levity, and Henry's attentions weary Fanny. Edmund and she find comfort in their friendship, and Jane Austen once more suggests how much more Edmund cares for Fanny than he admits even to himself, when he says:

'I have been talking incessantly all night, and with nothing to say. But with *you*, Fanny, there may be peace. You will not want to be talked to. Let us have the luxury of silence.' (*Chapter 28*)

The narrator's comment has an ironic flavour:

Fanny would hardly even speak her agreement . . . and they went down their two dances together with such sober tranquillity as might satisfy any looker-on, that Sir Thomas had been bringing up no wife for his younger son. (*Chapter 28*)

The 'looker-on' would have correctly assessed Sir Thomas's intention and Edmund's lack of self-knowledge but his is a short-sighted view. Fanny and Edmund may give no appearance of the agitation of lovers but their 'sober tranquillity' is very different from the demeanour of husbands and wives who are not suited to one another. We may very well suspect that this image of the human couple united in the hum-drum pleasure of the country dance is not far from Jane Austen's notion of the ideal marriage.

Fanny looks forward to having breakfast with William before he departs with Henry for London and the dinner with Admiral Crawford which may bring him promotion. The pleasure is tempered when Henry is invited too. The mingled happiness of the last hour with William is succeeded by that note of disintegration and loneliness which is struck so often in this novel. William and Henry leave for London; Edmund goes to Peterborough for his ordination:

It was a heavy, melancholy day . . . Nothing remained of last night but remembrances, which she had nobody to share in. (*Chapter 29*)

It is implied that the gentle tedium which follows the excitement of the ball will last for a long time. Now that Maria and Julia have moved to London, Lady Bertram thinks Fanny will be a member of their reduced circle for life: while Sir Thomas reads, they play cards.

Mary Crawford is less able than Fanny to endure the loss of people she loves. In her boredom and jealousy, she tries to get Fanny to tell her what Edmund thinks of her, but Fanny keeps a close guard on her tongue. Mary tries all the arts of arch exaggeration and droll insinuation to circumvent Fanny's composed propriety, when she says of Edmund:

'He is a very—a very pleasing young man himself, and I cannot help being rather concerned at not seeing him before I go to London . . . I should like to have seen him once more, I confess. But you must give my compliments to him.' (*Chapter 29*)

How is it that Jane Austen makes Mary Crawford so unattractive? Is it the insincere understatement of 'a very pleasing young man' and 'I cannot help being rather concerned at not seeing him'? In each phrase the studied detachment lightly conceals a stronger passion: we know—and Fanny knows—that Mary's interest in Edmund cannot properly be expressed in moderate terms.

Next day, Henry Crawford, secretive about his reason for visiting London, amazes Mary and the reader by announcing his intention to marry Fanny. Mary takes a malicious pleasure in the news: she 'was in a state of mind to rejoice in a connection with the Bertram family, and to be not displeased with her brother's marrying a little beneath him' (Chapter 30). Henry Crawford, having been almost a rake, is now reformed. He has fallen for Fanny's goodness. It is the tribute that vice, or recklessness, pays to virtue. As Mary puts it, 'Your wicked project upon her peace turns out a clever thought indeed. You will both find your good in it' (Chapter 30). There is, of course, no suggestion that Fanny will not accept him. But Henry's conversion to virtue is not altogether to be trusted. He is still fond of his reprobate uncle, and hopes Fanny will love him too. Mary, remembering 'her poor ill-used aunt', hopes that Henry's wife will have a better fate, but we cannot assume that Henry will be an ideal husband. The scene is now set for his proposal.  *Chap 31*

The concluding chapter of the second volume of the novel displays the conflict of Fanny's feelings as she finds herself moving into the trap which Henry and Sir Thomas have set for her. A letter from Mary signifies her approval. Sir Thomas talks of the joy she must be feeling; Henry Crawford thinks she owes him marriage in return for favours conferred; Mrs Norris talks of the expense she has caused her relatives. When she is alone, she can convince herself that Henry is not serious:

How could *she* have excited serious attachment in a man, who had seen so many, and been admired by so many, and flirted with so many, infinitely her superiors . . . who was every thing to every body, and seemed to find no one essential to him? (*Chapter 31*)

In that last judgment the essential narcissism of Henry is precisely caught. Henry is unimpressionable; his moral and emotional substance cannot feel the pressure, or take the stamp, of another human being. There is no place here for the fusion of mind and spirit which is what Fanny means by marriage.

## Volume Three (*Chapters 32–48*)

Next morning, Mr Crawford calls on Sir Thomas to declare his wish to marry Fanny. Sir Thomas, finding her in her room without a fire, suggests that the privations she has suffered have been miplaced: she is to enjoy a happier fate than she has been educated for. When Fanny astonishes him by saying he is mistaken about her feelings for Henry, Sir Thomas offers plausible reasons for accepting him, giving an objective assessment of Henry's advantages and reminding her of the obligations he has conferred upon her: he takes no account of her feelings and is unaware of any defects in Henry's character. What he says is wholly unrelated to the concept of love. Sir Thomas comes very close to suspecting Fanny's affections are already given elsewhere, but Fanny does not have to utter the denial which would have been a lie, and the moment passes, though she sees that she must look to her defences: 'She would rather die than own the truth, and she hoped by a little reflection to fortify herself beyond betraying it' (Chapter 32).

Obliquely, Sir Thomas has reassured himself that she is not in love with either of her cousins, but he now has no way of understanding her perverseness in refusing Henry Crawford. Since Fanny's dislike of Henry's character stems from his behaviour towards Maria and Julia, she cannot give a reasonable answer. She is disappointed to find that her uncle does not trust her judgment. Instead, he reads her a lecture on her wilfulness. In doing so he touches upon the status of women in the society of the time. Fanny's error consists in the fact that

> [She] can and will decide for [herself] . . . , without any consideration
> or deference for those who have surely some right to guide [her] — without even asking their advice (*Chapter 32*)

Sir Thomas uses every weapon of blackmail: she has not thought of the benefit her marriage would bring the family; or of the supreme value for a young woman of being 'settled for life'. Sir Thomas would not have expected Maria or Julia to refuse Mr Crawford — but they had a duty towards him as a father, which Fanny did not. Sir Thomas's speech is cruelly severe in implicitly withdrawing from Fanny the status he has recently accorded her as a member of his family.

Sir Thomas's manipulative harshness has produced misery — but perhaps also some relenting. He thinks the rest may be left to Mr Crawford's persuasiveness. But Fanny is adamant. Sir Thomas leaves her to herself, bereft of anyone in whom she might confide. When she returns to her room, she finds her uncle has ordered a fire to be lit. He needs no instruction in techniques of persuasion: sternness alternates with kindness; Fanny is isolated (even her aunts are not to be told of what has happened); she has been left to think of her physical and psychological dependence, and to repent of her ingratitude. But Sir Thomas is not merely a tyrannical manipulator. When Mrs Norris turns on Fanny unkindly, accusing her of faults he has levelled at her himself, Sir Thomas mentally dissociates himself from her views.

In the interview that follows with Henry Crawford (Chapter 33), Jane Austen displays her control of the presentation of events from different points of view. She shows us Henry as he appears in his own eyes, then turns to Fanny who characteristically wishes to say only what she means. We are also given the guidance of the narrative commentary which accurately analyses the nature of his affection. The 'warmth' which it ascribes to Henry suggests the energy of conquest; the 'delicacy' he lacks is a power of discriminating goals and purposes; while 'glory' is a more aggressively masculine, more overtly sexual version of the word 'triumph', so often used to describe the dominant posture of the victor in the social contests in these novels. After this damning judgment—it is a portrait of the wooer as conqueror—Henry is allowed to speak in his own indirectly presented words, in that rapid style of free indirect speech which Jane Austen so often uses to allow her characters to condemn themselves. We can imagine the phrases tumbling from his mouth:

> He would not despair: he would not desist. He had every well-grounded reason for solid attachment . . . (*Chapter 33*)

The third-person pronoun (first, of course, from the speaker's point of view) streams on until interrupted by an observation from the narrator: 'He knew not that he had a pre-engaged heart to attack. Of *that*, he had no suspicion.' The word 'attack' maintains the suggestion of aggressiveness already mentioned. Fanny is in the painful position of a woman in love who must protect her feelings from discovery. Far from not knowing her own mind (as her uncle has asserted), she knows it all too well.

Sir Thomas does everything he can to maintain the momentum of Henry's courtship by stressing its desirability. Yet even Sir Thomas sees that to persevere in the face of such discouragement is more wilful than discriminating. He tells Fanny she will not be persuaded to marry against her inclinations. But it remains his aim that she should marry well, and he does not believe another such offer is likely to be made to her. As Fanny puts it to herself:

> 'He who had married a daughter to Mr Rushworth. Romantic delicacy was certainly not to be expected from him.' (*Chapter 33*)

Although it remains unuttered, it is a telling criticism of Sir Thomas. 'Delicacy' is a word frequently used at this point in the novel: it means, 'the exquisite fineness of feeling, nicety of perception and sensitiveness of appreciation'. The delicacy which Henry attributes to Fanny (but which is not part of his own mental equipment) is not to be found in Sir Thomas either.

When Edmund returns he first approves of Henry's proposal, but closer observation raises doubts. Once again, Jane Austen uses conversation to probe intention and reveal character. Henry Crawford's impromptu reading of Shakespeare is fluent enough to impress the Bertram circle. The talk passes to the reading of prayers and the preaching of sermons. For once Henry Crawford is serious and Edmund sees a change of behaviour that might impress Fanny (Chapter 34). But Henry begins to give himself away: he is more concerned about the manner of conducting religious services than with their matter. He could not preach, 'but to the educated'. He 'must have a London audience'. He could imagine himself preaching 'once or twice in the spring . . . but not for a constancy; it would not do for a constancy'. Fanny is drawn into a conversation she tried to avoid. When she suggests he is describing his own instability, he does not deny it. There is an inherent absurdity in Henry's assessment of himself: though he swears constancy, he knows it is his unsteadiness that Fanny distrusts.

It falls to Edmund to attempt an assessment of Fanny's feelings. He knows her attachment to Mansfield; he knows how different Fanny and Henry are (Chapter 35). Henry is 'lively, and it may be a little unthinking' — 'Crawford's *feelings* . . . have hitherto been too much his guides.' Fanny would be a rock to which he could attach himself. Edmund urges Henry's claims as Mary's brother and his own possible brother-in-law. Everything points to Fanny's accepting him at last. And yet — as Fanny puts it — why should a man expect that his love will be returned? Marriage presupposes friendship and ties of common interest: it has nothing to do with the relentless pursuit Henry's courtship has become.

Fanny's next encounter is with Mary, who appears as the angry sister of Henry and the triumphant beloved of Edmund. Fanny is obliged to see her in the room where, three months before, she listened to Mary and Edmund rehearsing *Lovers' Vows*. Mary is not slow to recall the event and the power she has gained over Edmund. When Mary reveals that it was Henry's idea to give Fanny the necklace for the ball, Fanny is prompted to be frank about his character. Their habits of speech help to reveal the moral differences between them. Fanny's formal speech has a gravity which Mary's archness cannot match. Fanny's deliberate understatement suggests a moral as well as a syntactical control: she is the calm, clear-sighted observer who cannot be fooled. There is now a hint of vulgarity in Mary's speech, as if there has been a deliberate coarsening of the character by the author which finds expression in verbal terms. Next day, Mary and Henry leave for London.

Henry Crawford being disposed of as a suitor, what will become of Mary and Edmund? Edmund intends to follow the Crawfords to London: Fanny waits, and fears the worst. For her a further ordeal is in store: Sir Thomas believes some medicine is needed to correct his niece's understanding. She will return home to Portsmouth to learn 'the value of a good income' (Chapter 37). Initially, Fanny is delighted, though William suggests something of the reality she will meet by speaking of a house which 'is always in confusion'. The disorder is soon evident; Fanny's high hopes for Portsmouth are misplaced. Poverty and narrowness do not produce happiness; indifference, jealousy and aggressive self-assertion are not there restrained by any habit of decorum. Fanny has to admit that her home

. . . was the abode of noise, disorder, and impropriety. Nobody was in their right place, nothing was done as it ought to be. (*Chapter 39*)

There is another reason for Fanny's disappointment: she has no close links with her natural family, except for William. It would be a mistake to suppose that her attitude to Portsmouth is based on snobbery; while it is true that few compensating virtues are allowed to grow in this plot of poverty and mismanagement, it is not implied that the concept of order cannot be developed there. Fanny's experience at Portsmouth is in some respects a repetition in a different key of her experience at Mansfield. Different qualities of character are required to manage the affairs of this feckless household.

If women are subordinate to the men at Mansfield, at Portsmouth they have no position except as domestic managers. All that matters in the bustle and disorder is what must be done to satisfy immediate needs. There is no sense of perspective which would accommodate the needs and interests of all the family. Fanny cannot leave Portsmouth since she is dependent on her uncle for permission to return to Mansfield and for the means of doing so. From Mary Crawford, she hears something of what her cousins are doing in London, and she knows that Edmund has taken no irrevocable step. In the reduced circumstances of Portsmouth, Fanny tries to maintain the values of industry, consideration for others and the pursuit of cultural interests which she has been able to take for granted in her uncle's house. She finds in her sister, Susan, an apt pupil and companion.

The unexpected arrival of Henry Crawford temporarily embarrasses Fanny, but his contact with the family enhances the reputation of both Henry and Mr Price. In the presence of a gentleman, Fanny's father is stimulated to a display of his best manners, but, egotistically male, he absorbs Henry's attention, who, in turn, is able to show his tact and social address. Jane Austen knows how painful it is to conduct a delicate personal relationship in cramped, unsympathetic surroundings. The presence of Susan, sharp-eyed and intelligent, makes intimate conversation impossible.

When Henry leaves, Fanny has to depend once more on Mary's letters. She is glad that Mary is not able to report that Edmund has proposed to her, and properly disdainful of the good opinion of Mary's London friends have of him, based on six months' acquaintance. Now that Fanny knows that Edmund is in London, she waits impatiently for a letter from him. These pages of the novel are in some ways its most painful: they move slowly; Fanny is isolated, depressed, apprehensive of the effect Mary's social ambitions will have on Edmund's character. In this shadowy half-life, almost killed by the medicine meant to cure her dislike of Henry Crawford, she cultivates what is positive in her family.

When Edmund's letter arrives, it comes from Mansfield where he has returned, disappointed with his reception in London (Chapter 44): he has not proposed to Mary whom he found 'in high spirits, and surrounded by those who were giving all the support of their own bad sense to her too lively mind.' Beset by the evil influences of her London friends, all the familiar weaknesses of Mary's character are painfully exposed. Yet Edmund still believes 'she is the only woman in the world whom I could ever think of as a wife'. Edmund's letter is prolix and uncertain, displaying a degree of selfishness and indecision which can hardly raise him in the reader's estimation. His defence of Mary Crawford is difficult to reconcile with his perception of the less admirable aspects of her character revealed by her conversation and letters. The more damage Jane Austen has done to Mary's character in the course of the novel, the less we are able to sympathise with Edmund's inability to free himself from her influence.

A letter from Lady Bertram brings news of Tom's illness, the first of a series of events which suggest the value Fanny might be to Mansfield. For a moment the spectre of consumption is raised and Fanny sees that Edmund will be even more attractive to Mary as heir to Mansfield Park, if his brother dies. She mentally decides that 'Portsmouth was Portsmouth: Mansfield was home' (Chapter 45), but her delicacy prevents her confessing this discovery to her parents until she finds they do not mind. A further letter from Mary shows that the consequences of Tom's possible death have not been lost on her. A hint that Henry Crawford and Maria Rushworth have been seeing one another in London offers a clue to the surprise that Jane Austen is preparing for her characters. Mary repeats a previous offer to take Fanny back to Mansfield, but she cannot accept a favour from 'persons in whose feeling and conduct . . . she saw so much to condemn'. Gradually, the Crawfords are being brought into focus for a final judgment.

A further letter from Mary contains the first hint that something has gone wrong in London. A newspaper report suggests that Henry has eloped with Maria. Fanny is quick to imagine the full consequences of the scandal. It is a moment, perhaps, to contrast with Catherine Morland's perception that the things she had imagined in Northanger Abbey did not happen in 'the midland counties of England'. Here, Fanny Price is forced to acknowledge the range of moral disorder inherent in the 'common feelings of common life'. It is a culmination of the wayward and subversive habits of mind and of speech—that combination of liveliness and wilfulness—represented by the Crawfords and the Bertram girls, which Fanny has been aware of all through the novel.

A letter from Edmund breaks the news that Julia has eloped with Yates but also tells her that he is coming to take her back to Mansfield along with her younger sister Susan. Jane Austen writes finely of Fanny's mixed feelings and of the strange irony by which pleasure can be produced out of the pain of others:

> She was, she felt she was, in the greatest danger of being exquisitely happy, while so many were miserable. The evil which brought such good to her! She dreaded lest she should learn to be insensible of it. (*Chapter 46*)

But Fanny is equally aware of the danger of being diverted from what is good by too strong a sense of what is good for her. Her return to Mansfield gives her the keenest pleasure; we are reminded of the delight she takes in the beauty of the countryside. Her welcome home is of the warmest; for once Lady Bertram throws off her indolence and comes to greet her. But even in their present wretchedness, Mrs Norris finds a reason for blaming Fanny: if she had married Mr Crawford none of this would have happened.

It is clear that Edmund has now given up Mary Crawford but it is not for some days that he feels able to talk to Fanny about his feelings. When he does so it is clear that he has not the self-knowledge to resist the subtle wishes of his own egotism. Jane Austen's description of Edmund's confession is ironic, but the irony is tempered with sympathy:

> . . . with the usual beginnings, . . . and the usual declaration that if she would listen to him for a few minutes, he would be very brief, . . . he entered upon the luxury of relating circumstances and sensations of the first interest to himself, to one of whose affectionate sympathy he was quite convinced. (*Chapter 47*)

Edmund's capacity for distinguishing between what is good in itself and what is good for him is much feebler than Fanny's, and Jane Austen pins down his homespun vanity, his diffident good opinion of himself, with a sure touch.

When Edmund tells Fanny about his last interview with Mary, it is on her language that he dwells (Chapter 47). The words she uses to describe the behaviour of Henry and Maria seem inappropriate to its enormity: where Fanny and the Bertrams talk of 'guilt' and 'misery', Mary talks of 'folly'. Edmund sums up Mary with the remark, 'Hers are not faults of

temper . . . Hers are faults of principle . . . of blunted delicacy and a cor-
rupted, vitiated mind.' Mary has lost the power to distinguish the shades of
good and evil. What horrifies Edmund is that she had adopted an entirely
pragmatic approach to Henry and Maria's situation. She believes they must
not be separated, because if they are, there will be less chance of their
marrying. If they do marry, they may win back social acceptance. The
point at issue is whether acts are to be judged by their consequences, or by
an absolute standard of right and wrong. In Edmund's view Maria's adul-
terous elopement is a crime.

Slowly, Edmund's state of self-knowledge is being transformed. His
eyes have been opened to Mary's character; now the stage is set for him to
recognise his feelings for Fanny. Now, disarmingly, Jane Austen does not
trouble to conceal her partiality for her heroine. Fanny has so identified
herself with the right and the good that there can be no further denial of her
happiness. In the final chapter of the novel, Jane Austen rounds off her
tale, anxious to

> . . . quit such odious subjects as soon as I can, impatient to restore every
> body, not greatly in fault themselves, to tolerable comfort and to have
> done with all the rest. (*Chapter 48*)

It would be wrong to convey the impression that the final chapter of
the novel is a mere tying-up of loose ends. It is surely the most uncom-
promisingly severe division of characters into sheep and goats, into
punished and pardoned, in all Jane Austen's novels. Sir Thomas learns to
repent his want of parental care and insight. Maria Bertram is sent to join
Mrs Norris in a remote part of the country where they can be one another's
punishment. Jane Austen hopes that Henry Crawford will suffer from guilt
and remorse, there being no social penalty for the man who commits
adultery. The removal of the Grants to London allows Mary to be consoled
by her sister, who alone of all their family has maintained standards of
charity and good sense. For Fanny there is reserved the awakening of
Edmund's love.

If it is true to say that in her novels Jane Austen returns again and again to
the puzzling fact of the close association in human life of qualities which
are apparently incompatible, in this novel she forces herself to choose
between values which are equally dear to her. In *Mansfield Park* wit and
good sense, goodness and cleverness, constancy and 'liveliness' are puri-
fied from the rough amalgam in which they are found in nature and separated into starkly contrasted elements. It is perhaps this process of purifica-
tion which may turn readers against Fanny, however much they admire her
staunchness, her intelligence, her courageous sense of the need to defend
the integrity of the self from the demands of others, and from the blind
desires that spring from some undisciplined part of it. The process of puri-
fication can almost be seen in the construction of the novel: the complex

social interplay of the first volume gives way to a narrower focus, in Volume Two, upon Fanny and Henry, Mary and Edmund. In Fanny's battle to defend herself against Henry, and Edmund's heedless pursuit of Mary, the distinctions between good and evil behaviour are drawn more sharply. In Fanny's long passive wait in Volume Three to see the outcome of these issues, we see the vulnerability of goodness and the odds against it succeeding in a world of chance and disorder. Jane Austen makes it come out right in the end, and distributes justice in a way that satisfies her. But the sense of the power of malice and selfishness, of carelessness and chance remains strong. The destructive potentialities of suffering are as evident as its spiritual value: it is by the closest margin in *Mansfield Park* that goodness is more than its own reward.

# Chapter 6

# *Emma*: the self unmasked

## Introduction

Jane Austen was surely mistaken when she said, as quoted in her nephew's *Memoir*, 'I am going to take a heroine whom no one but myself will much like.' Emma Woodhouse is certainly snobbish, self-centred, condescending and manipulative; yet her vivacity, her capacity for self-deception and self-aggrandisement are both deplorable and attractive. The reader of *Mansfield Park* must be astonished at the mercy which Jane Austen has been able to extend in *Emma* to faults of character which were subjected to ruthless analysis and unsparing condemnation in the previous book. Without the self-knowledge which Emma acquires during the course of this novel, she might appear a monster, but she wins our sympathy by her capacity for shame and for a moral and intellectual growth which no character shows in *Mansfield Park*. (Edmund's process of learning in that novel is abject, in comparison.) Emma is a benign version of many of the female characters we have already met in the novels: Isabella Thorpe in *Northanger Abbey* and Lucy Steele in *Sense and Sensibility* are poor and distant relations, who show the most vulgar aspects of her self-assurance — their closest analogue in *Emma* is Mrs Elton. If Emma is of this sisterhood in some respects, her manner is more polished, the deplorable elements in her character more deeply hidden, her essential virtues more abundant and generous. She is closer to Mary Crawford in *Mansfield Park*, warm, outgoing, accomplished, attractive but morally flawed, and closer still to Elizabeth Bennet in *Pride and Prejudice*. What is it about these three characters which entitles them to different treatment? Despite her acknowledgement of Mary's qualities, Jane Austen pursues her faults relentlessly. To Elizabeth and to Emma she is generous and forgiving: both of them show a capacity to learn, both know that it is sometimes wise to be serious. They are not incurable; even their most radically unsatisfactory faults of character are capable of change. For this reason alone, any dislike we may have of them must be tempered with admiration; for imperfect characters, such as ourselves, they are a sign of hope.

# Commentary

## Volume One (*Chapters 1–18*)

At the beginning of the novel there is an emptiness in Emma's life: Miss Taylor, her teacher, companion and friend has just been married, and, although Emma claims credit for bringing the newly-weds together, it has left a vacuum in her life which cannot be filled by her married sister who lives in London or by her father, who is too old and too obsessed with his health, to offer her companionship. Jane Austen loses no time in suggesting some of the dangers to which Emma is now exposed: although she had been Emma's governess, Miss Taylor's mildness of temper 'had hardly allowed her to impose any restraint'; Emma 'directed chiefly by her own [judgment]' had been 'doing just what she liked' (Chapter 1). The element of wilfulness in Emma's character may be compared with her father's

> . . . habits of gentle selfishness and of never being able to suppose that other people could feel differently from himself. (*Chapter 1*)

As we soon discover, Emma, too, shares some of this moral blindness. Mr Woodhouse's conviction that everyone shares his opinion is harmless, indeed ridiculous, since it applies to trivial aspects of human behaviour. Emma is a more dangerous example of the same disability: she is willing to believe that she knows better than others and can manage their lives better than they could. In their first conversation in the novel, Mr Knightley reproaches her for claiming to have arranged Miss Taylor's marriage. When Emma claims that her plans have been crowned with success, Mr Knightley replies:

> 'I do not understand what you mean by 'success' . . . Success supposes endeavour. Your time has been properly and delicately spent, if you have been endeavouring for the last few years to bring about this marriage. A worthy employment for a young lady's mind!' (*Chapter 1*)

Mr Knightley's is the voice of reason in the world. He kindly but firmly pours cold water on Emma's fantasies. There can be no merit in idle speculation, but Emma's fantasies feed her delusions of power. Her interference denies others their independence, indeed their full adulthood, as Mr Knightley implies, when he says of the next object of her attention, Mr Elton:

> 'Invite him to dinner, Emma, and help him to the best of the fish and the chicken, but leave him to chuse his own wife.' (*Chapter 1*)

For all her liveliness and wit, Emma has not grasped the difference between a moral and a non-moral choice. Choosing what to eat is a matter of taste, choosing a wife is a complex act, which is an implicit avowal of the values of the agent.

Emma demonstrates her ignorance of the seriousness of such a commitment by filling the gap in her life with a young woman called Harriet Smith for whom she plans a marriage with the local clergyman, Mr Elton. Harriet, the illegitimate daughter of someone unknown, is attached to a group of characters located in the village of Highbury which lies at the centre of the imaginary geographical area in which the novel is set, bordered by Hartfield, the Woodhouse's estate, which is 'but a sort of notch in the Donwell Abbey estate', which belongs to Mr Knightley. Randalls, the estate which Mr Weston bought after realising 'an easy competence' (Chapter 2) in trade is part of the parish of Highbury, whose vicar is the Reverend Philip Elton. We soon become familiar with the streets of the town, where stand the Crown Inn, the house where Miss Bates and her mother live, and Ford's shop, 'first in size and fashion in the place'.

The garrulous Miss Bates, her mother and Mrs Goddard, the school mistress, at whose school Harriet Smith resides, gain what social distinction they possess from their usefulness to Mr Woodhouse as dinner guests or card-players. Emma is attracted by Harriet's good looks but more particularly by her deference. Harriet showed

> . . . so proper and becoming a deference, seeming so pleasantly grateful for being admitted to Hartfield, and so artlessly impressed by the appearance of every thing in so superior a style to what she had been used to, that she must have good sense and deserve encouragement. Encouragment should be given. Those soft blue eyes and all those natural graces should not be wasted on the inferior society of Highbury and its connections. The acquaintance she had already formed were unworthy of her. (*Chapter 3*)

Although no explicit signal of the fact has been given, the narrative voice has now moved so close to the point of view of Emma herself that we can almost detect her tone of voice in the narrative itself, most clearly so in the last two sentences of the quotation. It is another instance of Jane Austen's use of the technique of 'free indirect speech' which we first met in *Northanger Abbey*. Given the disparity of their social position, we may not be too concerned that what Emma first picks out for approval in Harriet is her deference, but Emma's dwelling on her gratitude reveals a less than admirable appetite for subservience. Her awareness of, and pleasure in, her own superiority and the 'superior' appearance of Hartfield begin to sound complacent, even vulgar. Her unthinking conclusion that Harriet's school friends 'must be doing her harm' (Chapter 3) is surely intended to strike us as odious. Emma has no doubt about her capacity to improve Harriet, and we know from *Mansfield Park* that Jane Austen may have some reservations about the value of 'improvement'.

When the narrative voice resumes its independence, Jane Austen makes no comment on what we have just heard. It is essential to the plan of the novel that the central character should not lose the narrator's good will. She is the heroine of the novel: adverse comment may be left to the reader. The narrator notes only her energy and the zest with which she carries out her duties as a hostess, but the terms in which these qualities are described deserve close attention. Consider Jane Austen's description of Emma as she tends to the needs of the ladies whom she has collected to enliven one of her father's dull evenings, among them Harriet Smith who has been brought along by Mrs Goddard:

> With an alacrity beyond the common impulse of a spirit which yet was never indifferent to the credit of doing everything well and attentively, with the real good-will of a mind delighted with its own ideas, did she then do all the honours of the meal . . . (*Chapter 3*)

The narrative suggests the enthusiasm which Emma brings to the task of looking after her guests, while recording the pleasure she takes in having her attentiveness admired; her goodwill is real but it is generated by self-congratulation and a deep-seated complacency. The narrator's apparent acceptance of traits which may have begun to offend the reader is carefully hedged by ambiguous phrases, which suggest that limiting judgments lurk underneath the narrator's apparent approval or toleration. And yet from another point of view, Emma's estimate of the evening's success has been shared by the excited Harriet Smith:

> . . . the humble, grateful little girl went off with highly gratified feelings, delighted with the affability with which Miss Woodhouse had treated her all the evening, and actually shaken hands with her at last! (*Chapter 3*)

The last phrase is a good example of 'free indirect speech', where the pressure of Harriet's excitement breaks out into words which she might have used, making havoc with the grammar of the sentence but conveying the delighted awe with which Harriet responds to Emma's patronage. For a moment our doubts about Emma's intentions may be disarmed: why should we make objections on Harriet's behalf when she is so pleased with her welcome?

Jane Austen establishes our interest in her novel by these sophisticated manipulations of the point of view. Emma and Harriet are able to form a relationship because each is flattered by the other's attention. Harriet, of course, has no knowledge of Emma's plans for her, and Emma knows nothing of Harriet's personal history; she attaches no importance to the network of social relationships into which Harriet has already entered. She sees Harriet as a piece of plastic material whose future shape she will determine. Jane Austen's fictional technique allows her to suggest the distinct inner worlds of individuals who have a keen sense of their own intentions but a limited insight into the consciousness of the other. In part, this fictional world resembles the world of limited egotistical vision which we all know, but since we are allowed insight into more than one consciousness, we gain a greater sense of the limitations of the individual point of view.

Jane Austen stresses Harriet's usefulness to Emma; she serves as a walking companion, she is 'exactly the something which her home required' (Chapter 4)—a phrase that surely implies a severe criticism of Emma's instrumental view of Harriet. Emma means to be useful to Harriet, but there is no reciprocity about the relationship: Emma remains the judge of what the term will mean. The first hint of doubt about the completeness of their knowledge of one another is raised by Harriet's relationship with the Martins. Emma is first amused, then alarmed, by Harriet's interest in the family, especially in the unmarried farmer's son. She is swift to indicate her own lack of interest:

> A young farmer . . . can need none of my help, and is therefore in one sense as much above my notice as in every other he is below it. (*Chapter 4*)

Emma's language soon transforms Mr Robert Martin from an individual to a type; the real nature of her relationship to Harriet is precisely, indeed cruelly, defined. To be counted as someone to whom Emma can be useful, Harriet must trade her own independence for the patronage of her social superior. Emma shows here a touch of Lady Catherine in *Pride and Prejudice*: her patronage is less assertive, her manners more winning, but those who do not submit to her control are beneath her notice. It becomes clear that Emma expects Harriet to keep the young farmer at a distance. Her undisguised snobbery is oblivious to any real feeling Harriet may have for her friends. When they meet him on their walk, he is immediately compared to his disadvantage with real gentlemen, but it is only to Mr Knightley—the exemplar of the novel's moral ideal—that Harriet finds him inferior. Emma's canons of judgment are superficial by comparison: because Mr Martin is interested in his trade, he is likely to grow rich, but remain illiterate and coarse, in her view. (A prejudice against trade has not been a sign of a generous intelligence in earlier novels.) His preference for the Agricultural Reports over the Gothic romances which Emma admires sets him down as a dullard. He will not do for Harriet. Mr Elton, on the other hand, who was 'really a very pleasing young man, a young man whom any woman not fastidious might like' (Chapter 4), will be a suitable husband for Harriet, just as she will be good enough for him. Emma does not approve of Mr Elton absolutely—he has too many defects to satisfy her —but he will do well enough for Harriet.

There is no need for the narrator to underline the effrontery of Emma's behaviour: her own judgments indicate how little respect she has for those she claims to be helping. It is for the reader to decide how much censure she deserves for playing with the lives of people she scarcely knows. The issues are debated in Chapter 5 in a conversation between Mr Knightley and Mrs Weston on the friendship between Emma and Harriet, in which Knightley's sharply critical estimate of Emma's wilfulness is contrasted with Mrs Weston's belief in her capacity for kindness and love. Both agree that Emma is beautiful and free from personal vanity. Mr Knightley, however, does not believe that Emma knows herself; he doesn't believe she will enable Harriet to 'adapt herself rationally to the varieties of her situation in life.' These two witnesses are essential to the success of Jane Austen's purposes at this early stage of the novel. Mrs Weston ('poor Miss Taylor' that was) is established in the first chapter as a wise, if partial, woman who has been Emma's governess and is now her friend. Although she glosses over her defects, her testimony to other aspects of Emma's character is essential to our willingness to remain patient with Emma. From his first appearance in the novel, Knightley has brought a robustly analytical mind to Emma's defects, but it is quite clear that he thinks her worth caring about, although there is no hint that he is personally interested in her. Indeed Mrs Weston hopes that Emma will some day marry her husband's son by a previous marriage.

The match which Emma promotes between Harriet and Mr Elton is handled with a wonderful lightness of touch. Mr Elton's character is soon revealed in the banality of his speech. He is deferential to Emma, finding nothing more striking to say than to repeat her phrases with a mechanically judicious, 'Exactly so' (Chapter 6). Part of the comedy arises from the exactitude with which events in the real world appear to match Emma's plans: Mr Elton's enthusiasm for her drawings can only be accounted for by his love for Harriet, who is to sit for one. Whatever criticisms may be made of the drawing, Mr Elton defends it and is pleased to take it to London to be framed. Whatever compliments he addresses to Emma spring, she is sure, from his love for Harriet.

The swirl of gallantry which the portrait generates is soon dashed by some genuine feelings: a proposal of marriage by Robert Martin has to be fended off. Emma is surprised to find that his letter to Harriet 'would not have disgraced a gentleman' (Chapter 7). Her assumption that Harriet will refuse him fails to take account of Harriet's real feelings for him. When her silence is not enough to resolve Harriet's doubts about what to do, she prompts her to remember Mr Elton. When Harriet struggles towards the refusal Emma has pointedly refrained from advising her to make, Emma indicates what acceptance would have meant:

> 'It would have grieved me to lose your acquaintance, which must have been the consequence of your marrying Mr Martin . . . I could not have visited Mrs Robert Martin of Abbey-Mill Farm. Now I am secure of you forever.' (*Chapter 7*)

Mr Knightley's disapproval of the friendship is justified by this example of Emma's selfish possessiveness and by the false opinion she gives Harriet of her own importance. ('Dear affectionate creature!' She tells her. 'You banished to Abbey-Mill Farm! — *You* confined to the society of the illiterate and vulgar all your life!') Harriet has a capacity for affection, though she lacks the power of mind to understand what she feels. Emma is too intelligent to be so blind; she has not been able to persuade herself that Martin's proposal of marriage was not his own work; she knows that it cannot be dismissed because it is 'short', since honest intention and sincere feeling need not be expressed at length, but her social prejudice is too impenetrable to count it as evidence that Martin is not an ignorant man. She has forced Harriet to stifle her frail but genuine feelings for him, which, tinged now with guilt, continue to haunt her until Emma dispels them with fantasies about Mr Elton.

Mr Knightley's view of Robert Martin, based on acquaintance rather than prejudice, is very different. His 'short decided answers' (Chapter 8) to Mr Woodhouse's protracted but pointless civilities offer an apt comparison with the conciseness of Robert Martin's proposal. Mr Knightley has been consulted about the matter: he approves of Robert Martin and vigorously repudiates the idea that he is not Harriet's equal. Knightley's view of Harriet is trenchant and downright: he begins with her social and financial position and continues with her personal merits. He assumes that the appraisal of a woman's eligibility for marriage should be made on a rational basis, though he allows that the man's affection will play a deciding part in the final judgment. We may accept his account of Harriet's weaknesses even if we credit her with a sincerity of feeling unknown to him. Emma argues that they are socially incompatible. Harriet has more advantage than Knightley allows for, particularly in looks, which men value most. She even suggests that it is on those grounds that Knightley will choose his own wife. Knightley disagrees: men choose their wives on the rational grounds of social advantage or personal merit. Harriet's expectations are only of Emma's making: if she is made to think too much of herself, she will be unhappy. If Emma is thinking of Mr Elton as a husband for Harriet, she is mistaken:

> Elton [says Mr Knightley] may talk sentimentally, but he will act rationally. He is as well acquainted with his own claims, as you can be with Harriet's. (*Chapter 8*)

Emma's answer to these hard-headed observations is a complex piece of deception. In denying that she means to promote a marriage between Elton and Harriet she deceives herself as well as Knightley. She has no real wish to look steadily at the truth of Harriet's position. What Knightley says about Elton frightens her a little but ready rationalisations come to her aid: Mr Elton is more passionate than prudent, and in any case he could not be credited with more than 'a reasonable, becoming degree of prudence.' It is as if she believes that Mr Elton's prudence would be limited by the deference he would feel was due to her. She is happy to be reassured by Harriet's report of Mr Elton's visit to London, which has excited the gossips of Highbury.

Events begin to move as Emma has imagined. Chapter 9 finds Emma and Harriet engaged in a search for riddles, to which Mr Elton contributes a verse on courtship. Despite Elton's pointed delivery of the riddle to Emma, she is convinced it is meant for Harriet. It is the justification she had been looking for against the doubts of Mr Knightley. Emma exults in her success ('This is an attachment which a woman may well feel pride in creating. This is a connection which offers nothing but good') even as she admits the strangeness with which her fantasies have come true. Despite her firm assertions to the contrary, she has been engaged in match-making all the time. There is a note of dreadful presumption about her assertion that Hartfield controverts Shakespeare's notion that the course of true love does not run smooth, as if Emma knew better than the playwright. Harriet's feelings do not quite desert her: though she feels all the wonder of the idea that Mr Elton should be in love with her, there is something painfully comic about her belief that Mr Elton's way of declaring his love is better than that of the man who has 'very good sense in a common way, like everybody else' and who writes a letter to 'say what [he] must, in a short way.' Once again, Jane Austen makes her grasp a distinction without seeing its significance.

The following chapter (Chapter 10) offers a detailed account of Emma's efforts to bring Mr Elton to the point of proposing to Harriet. Despite her certainty about his intentions, Mr Elton is oddly resistant to more than small talk with Harriet. But the chapter is not simply an account of frustrated expectations: it also contains Emma's meditation on marriage. She values her independence too much to be anxious to marry, but her reflections on becoming an old maid mix shrewdness and self-deception. When she speaks of her own resources of mind and hand, and of the blessings she expects from her nephews and nieces, she might be Jane Austen speaking of herself. But on the evidence of the novel, Emma has not the perseverance to manage the resources she hopes she can draw upon in middle age. For Emma, poverty is the main danger for the unmarried woman, yet Miss Bates, the nearest example of the spinster of slender means, scarcely fits her picture of the embittered, middle-aged old maid. But Emma manages to turn Miss Bates's virtues against her and is bored by the thought of Jane Fairfax, her niece. With disdainful disparagements of her friends on her lips, Emma hurries to Highbury to relieve the distresses of the poor.

The arrival of Mr and Mrs John Knightley and their five children interrupts the course of Harriet's and Mr Elton's supposed love affair. Mr Woodhouse's daughter and son-in-law share some of the qualities of their sister and brother. In Isabella, Emma's imaginativeness is modified by her sister's comparative lack of intelligence, by her fretful absorption in the cares of motherhood and by a taste for hypochondria which she shares with her father. In John Knightley, his brother's intellectual severity is degraded into a rigid and sometimes ungracious concern for matters of fact. But whatever their inadequacies, the Knightleys revel in domesticity: they make it clear how much is to be endured for the sake of family affection. Emma's disagreement with Knightley over Harriet cannot survive the arrival of their nephew and nieces. Indeed, it is with her family that Emma's qualities are seen to advantage. With them, she is diplomatic, heading off topics which she knows are dangerous, and the readiness with which Mr George Knightley helps her to keep explosive family feelings under control shows the closeness of their understanding.

The concluding events of Volume One of the novel begin with an invitation to dinner at Randalls which Harriet cannot take up because she is suffering from 'a sore throat': Mr Elton is immediately fearful of its being infectious, but Emma is surprised he does not stay at home himself, in sympathy with Harriet. Now the narrator tells us directly that Emma is 'too eager and busy in her own previous conceptions and views to hear him impartially, or see him with clear vision' (Chapter 13). When Mr John Knightley, a hitherto uninvolved third party, suggests that Mr Elton may be in love with her, and that her behaviour may have encouraged him, the idea is indignantly brushed aside.

The comedy of egotism lies in its inability to look beyond the present state of the self: Mr Woodhouse, constitutionally terrified of draughts, consents to go out on a night that threatens snow, because he is

> . . . too full of the wonder of his own going, and the pleasure it was to afford at Randalls to see that it was cold, and too well wrapt up to feel it.
> (*Chapter 13*)

Mr Elton can think only fleetingly of Harriet as he is carried to dinner 'so fenced and guarded from the weather, that not a breath of air can find its way unpermitted' (Chapter 13). Only Mr John Knightley, who is a lawyer, preserves a crusty sense of the risks they are running. Jane Austen's attitude to the self-centredness of her characters is ambivalent: she accepts the importance of 'all those little matters on which the daily happiness of private life depends' (Chapter 14). But she is keenly aware of the need to discipline these competing obsessions so that they will not damage one another in the blind pursuit of personal interest. Mr Elton's intentions may have more relevance to Emma than she supposes, just as Emma's own wish to see Frank Churchill, Mr Weston's son, depends entirely on the whim of his aunt, who 'has no more heart than a stone to people in general' (Chapter 14). The consideration of Frank Churchill's relationship to his family evokes from Emma the concept of duty: it is clear to her what he 'ought' to do, though Mrs Weston remarks that only a close consideration of his circumstances will throw light on what Frank can do. Emma clearly believes that a young man has more power than a young woman to do what he wants, but, according to Mrs Weston, Mrs Churchill of Enscombe is above any general rule of conduct—'*she* is so very unreasonable, and every thing gives way to her' (Chapter 14). When Emma suggests what Frank ought to do, she is no doubt thinking of her own interests, while Mrs Weston allows her more generous sympathy to dwell on the actual circumstances of the young man's life. But at least the inconvenient consequences of caprice have been recognised and the possibility of doing one's duty has been raised.

When the gentlemen leave the dinner table to join the ladies, Emma's fears that Mr Elton may have an interest in her are renewed. He is not only concerned that Emma might catch Harriet's cold, he begins to assert a right to be concerned for her welfare which is not to her taste. The awkwardness is resolved by the discovery that it is snowing, and the party begins to break up. Mr Woodhouse is only too keen to return; Isabella, worried for her children, is ready to leave her father and sister behind, provided she can get home herself. Mr John Knightley takes pleasure in recalling his own forebodings about the weather and in congratulating his father-in-law on his courage in venturing out. It is Mr George Knightley who takes practical steps to judge their position and settle with Emma what should be done. The natural concern of John Knightley to be with his wife leaves Emma alone in her brother-in-law's carriage with a slightly drunk Mr Elton.

His outpourings on 'the subject of his own passion' (Chapter 15) are all that we would expect. Mr Elton has had no eyes for Harriet; in his own opinion he has been quite consistent:

'Every thing that I have said or done, for many weeks past, has been with the sole view of marking my adoration of yourself.' (*Chapter 15*)

It is characteristic of the subjective point of view that it regards its opinions to be valid for everyone. It is at the point of intersection between two such opinions—each blind to the other but confident of being recognised—that Jane Austen finds the largest scope for her comedy.

Now, Emma discovers that she has been mistaken; briefly, she glimpses herself as Mr Elton has seen her, and he as he has been seen by her; the gap between their expectations and reality is ludicrous. In her extremity, Emma's self-command—and her command of language—does not desert her; she treats Mr Elton to a fearsome display of the temper of her class:

'Encouragement!—I give you encouragement!—sir, you have been entirely mistaken in supposing it. I have seen you only as the admirer of my friend.' (*Chapter 15*)

Mr Elton's repudiation of an interest in Harriet has been precisely on the grounds of social inequality predicted by Mr Knightley. Emma returns the compliment by spurning his own claim to social equality with herself. But Emma's superb control of language should not blind us to her manipulation of the truth. Harriet *has* been misled by Emma herself. It is not the case, as she implies, that only Mr Elton will be disappointed. She has put down Mr Elton and raised Harriet to the elevated social sphere she occupies herself. It is an affront Mr Elton will not forgive, and it makes no difference to the reality of Harriet's status. As Emma well knows, only a husband can alter that. In fact, Emma's impenetrable social poise conceals feelings of 'pain and humiliation' which she is left to suffer in private. In this first major recoil upon herself, Emma demonstrates the difference between the outward control of the poised social performer and the uncertainty of the private woman. It is to Emma's credit that her first thought is for Harriet (Chapter 16). Now she sees what she has done: 'She has taken up the idea [of Elton's preference for Harriet] — and made everything bend to it.' She had supposed that his attentions to herself were simply a sign that 'with all the gentleness of his address, true elegance was sometimes wanting.' (It is this phrase which the Oxford English Dictionary uses to illustrate that 'elegance' means 'refinement in manners and taste.') Faced with his effrontery in proposing to her, Emma makes her own retrospective judgment of Elton's behaviour. Looking at it from her own point of view, she can easily see that it has everything to do with self-advancement, nothing to do with love. She is compelled to admit that Mr Knightley and his brother were right about Mr Elton and that her own opinion was wrong. It is just such passages of self-criticism which prevent Emma being seen as a monstrous figure of snobbery, self-deception and manipulation. But it is still the case that it is easier for her to recognise truths of this kind when her own interests are involved than when she is considering the interests of others. One further point in Emma's favour is that she does make an effort to look at recent events from Mr Elton's point of view. In this light, she is compelled to acknowledge that she must have appeared to encourage him. In conclusion, she blames herself:

> The first error and the worst lay at her door. It was foolish, it was wrong, to take so active a part in bringing any two people together. It was adventuring too far, assuming too much, making light of what ought to be serious, a trick of what ought to be simple. She was quite concerned and ashamed, and resolved to do such things no more. (*Chapter 16*)

Emma fails to keep her resolve, but she has identified the fundamental ground of her error — the 'making light of what ought to be serious.' She finds some doubtful comfort in the belief that the principal actors in the drama are not sensitive enough to feel the situation as keenly as she does, but she is aware that a painful interview with Harriet must take place. When it does, Emma is impressed by Harriet's humility and simplicity. But the power of entering sympathetically into Harriet's feelings fails her: she can easily see reasons for Harriet ceasing to love Mr Elton—it is logical that she should do so—it is beyond her power to imagine why she should continue to do so.

The first volume of the novel ends in anti-climax. Mr Elton leaves hurriedly for Bath, but Frank Churchill's visit to Highbury does not take place. When Emma and Mr Knightley discuss the matter, Emma recapitulates Mrs Weston's arguments: no judgment can be made without detailed knowledge of the young man's situation. It is surely not without significance that Knightley argues as Emma had, in discussing the matter with Mrs Weston: Frank Churchill had a duty to visit his father, and a young man of independent means would find some way of carrying it out. Principles ought to be stronger than the wishes of the influential. Even Mrs Weston must feel slighted by the neglect of someone she must think of as a son. Frank Churchill may be an agreeable young man but he lacks 'English delicacy towards the feelings of other people' (Chapter 18). 'Delicacy' is a word we have met many times in *Mansfield Park*; it shares with 'elegance' the meaning of 'a refined sense of consideration for the feelings of others.' Their discussion ends in pique on Mr Knightley's part and puzzlement on Emma's. She acknowledges a prejudice for Frank Churchill, but she has never before known Mr Knightley to be blind to the merits of another. It is left to the reader to detect a hint of jealousy in Knightley's demeanour, and to notice that Emma's delight in argument may sometimes mask her true opinions even from herself. It is part of Jane Austen's strategy to contrive situations in the novel which suggest that for all their differences Knightley and Emma share an affinity—a wholly unconscious reliance on one another's good sense and a greater agreement in things that matter than either realises.

---

## Volume Two (*Chapters 19–36*)

---

The hope of offering Harriet some distraction leads Emma to visit Mrs and Miss Bates despite 'all the horror of being in danger of falling in with the second and third rate of Highbury, who were calling on them for ever' (Chapter 19). The accents are Emma's, of course, one element in whose attitude to Mrs Bates and her daughter is the fact that they lodge in a house which 'belonged to people in business.' We have already in a sense met Mrs and Miss Bates, although this is the first time we have heard Miss Bates talk. Her character is one of the triumphs of Jane Austen's imagination. Miss Bates's speech is a flood of disorganised utterances, tenuously linked. The distaste for Jane Fairfax, which Emma uncharitably expressed in an earlier chapter, is swamped by the endless warmth of her aunt's affection, who has no thought that her interest in her niece may not be shared by everyone. On this occasion, Miss Bates's rambling discourse is intended as an introduction to a reading of her niece's letter, but the substance of it (that

Jane has caught a cold and, instead of going to visit a recently married friend in Ireland, has chosen to visit her aunt and grandmother) is poured out in a hectic torrent of sentences which encompasses Mrs Bates's excellent eyesight, her defective hearing, Jane's handwriting, and the impossibility of accepting free medical treatment from Mr Perry. Her talk contains the hint that there had been a close friendship between Jane and the newly-married husband and that her friend, Miss Campbell, his bride, though 'elegant and amiable' had 'always been absolutely plain.' The chapter is both an extended joke against Emma, whose escape from Mr Elton to Miss Bates is from the frying pan to the fire, and an extended opportunity for Jane Austen to display her mastery of Miss Bates's disorganised thought patterns, which remind us that a simple kind of goodness is open to people of humble status and moderate intelligence.

Jane Fairfax, an orphan who has been brought up by a brother-officer of her dead father, beautiful, talented and elegant as she is, must now seek the only employment open to her, a post as a governess, a career she regards as her 'path of duty' (Chapter 20). The narrator leaves us in no doubt about her attitude to the step she is about to take:

> . . . she had now reached the age which her own judgment had fixed on for beginning. She had long resolved that one-and-twenty should be the period. With the fortitude of a devoted noviciate, she had resolved at one-and-twenty to complete the sacrifice, and retire from all the pleasures of life, of rational intercourse, equal society, peace and hope, to penance and mortification for ever. (*Chapter 20*)

One cannot be sure how far this deeply pessimistic view of the future that confronts Jane is endorsed by the narrator; the terms in which it is couched suggest that there is something too extreme in Jane's view of her fate, though there is nothing later in the novel to counter the suggestion that becoming a governess would be disagreeable. There is certainly a marked contrast between Jane's expectation of dependence and Emma's of independence. Emma can neither like Jane Fairfax, nor justify her dislike: some mixture of jealousy and guilt may account for her feeling. Jane exemplifies the standard of feminine accomplishment which Emma professes to admire, but her vulgar relatives and her own puzzling reserve create a prejudice in Emma's mind, which is reinforced by the romance she has begun to weave round Jane and Mr Dixon. Emma is sure that something is being concealed; and she is annoyed that Jane has nothing to say about Mr Frank Churchill, whom she has met while on holiday with her friends in Weymouth.

Whatever Emma's feelings, she keeps them private, being commended by Mr Knightley for her kindness to Jane. He has some news for her, but is forestalled by Miss Bates who has come with Jane to Hartfield to thank the Woodhouses for their gift of a leg of pork and to announce the approaching marriage of Mr Elton to a 'Miss Hawkins of Bath' (Chapter 21). Jane Austen orchestrates the conversation which follows so that Mr Woodhouse's reservations, Emma's curiosity, and Jane Fairfax's indifference serve as decoration to Miss Bates's characteristically benign account of the addition she expects to the excellence of Highbury society—a recital which Emma rather rudely interrupts. Miss Bates herself is inadvertently tactless in revealing some knowledge of Mr Elton's aspirations to marry Emma, which she does not think ridiculous. Emma is afraid that Harriet will hear the news before she has time to prepare her, but, when they meet, Harriet is more concerned about a chance meeting with Robert Martin and his sister. From her lengthy description of the encounter, however abortive, it is clear there remains some real feeling on both sides. Emma finds herself giving Harriet the news of Mr Elton's marriage more rapidly than she meant, perhaps so that Harriet's jealousy of Mr Elton's new wife may banish the Martins from her mind. Once more, Emma has been guilty of ignoring the value of the 'real feeling' and 'genuine delicacy' which the Martins have shown. She still believes (or pretends to believe) that Robert Martin's interest in Harriet springs from a wish to improve his social position. She further discredits the evidence of genuine affection between the parties by persuading herself that Harriet is too stupid to have made an accurate judgment about the events she has reported.

Jane Austen heralds the return of Mr Elton and his bride-to-be to Highbury with one of her most astringent sentences:

> Human nature is so well disposed towards those who are in interesting situations, that a young person, who either marries or dies, is sure of being kindly spoken of. (*Chapter 22*)

There is just a suggestion here that the common events of everyday life do not call forth such charity, and that malice and depreciation are more usual features of public comment. Emma is not impressed by his wife-to-be whose connections with trade are enough to discredit her. In comparison with Harriet, she is nothing, apart from her dowry and the fact that her sister keeps two carriages. Emma is not able to erase Harriet's interest in Mr Elton, who is stamped on her imagination and cannot easily be removed. To cure her of Mr Elton, she falls back on the Martin family, hoping that a carefully managed visit, which will indicate the limit to be set on their friendship, will deflect Harriet from Mr Elton while avoiding a renewal of her interest in Robert Martin.

Harriet is impressionable, unable to throw off the control which present circumstances have over her mind: even the sight of Mr Elton's trunk is enough to overwhelm her with a sense of what she has lost. But the road which leads to the Martins' farm has the same power to re-awaken an interest in her old friends. Emma can see the feelings which have been aroused and is sufficiently sensitive to wish that she could spare Harriet the pain of another separation from her friends, but she believes she must persevere.

Her weary spirits are revived by the news of Frank Churchill's impending arrival, which coincides with the coming of spring. The meeting of Emma and Frank Churchill, who has surprised and impressed them by arriving a day earlier than he had intended, is managed with great ease and mutual pleasure: does Frank Churchill know of the local expectation that he will fall in love with Emma? She is glad that her father appears quite unconscious of any such hope, but she is glad to have met this handsome young man, who now, with some apparent reluctance, plans to call as a matter of duty on Jane Fairfax whom he met in Weymouth.

Through Frank Churchill's interest we are now introduced to the daily life of Highbury. Jane Austen offers a good deal of evidence about her character's interests, which is sometimes given an immediate interpretation by Emma but which is also open to the interpretation of the reader, who may see more than any of the participants in the tale. It is obvious that Frank Churchill's interest in Highbury is stronger than is warranted by his association with Randalls or his presumed interest in Hartfield. Emma concludes that the accusation made of him of indifference to his native place and natural family has been unfair. But his plan to promote dancing at the Crown Inn suggests to her that he is not sufficiently aware of the danger of mixing different social groups:

> He seemed to have all the life and spirit, cheerful feelings and social inclination of his father, and nothing of the pride or reserve of Enscombe. Of pride, indeed, there was perhaps, scarcely enough; his indifference to a confusion of rank bordered too much on inelegance of mind. He could be no judge, however, of the evil he was holding cheap. It was but an effusion of lively spirits. (*Chapter 24*)

The judgment is Emma's, but we know from earlier novels that 'lively spirits' are not a sign of moral health, though we cannot take Emma's views simply at face value. If 'elegance of mind', for example, implies too careful a concern for the preservation of social distinctions, is it necessarily a virtue? It may seem at this point that one of the key-words of the novel has begun to develop a troublesome ambiguity: there is a kind of fastidiousness which may inhibit honest goodwill. When the conversation is resumed, we are reminded of the complexity of casual conversation: what is the point of this rapid, free-flowing dialogue, whose apparent subject is Jane Fairfax? In part, they are using Jane to establish their own relationship. Emma acknowledges her reservations about Jane which arise partly from jealousy of her talents, partly from a dislike of her wish for privacy. Emma is frank — or unwary — enough to reveal her suspicions about the tender feelings she suspects Jane has for her friend's husband. Only on a second reading can we appreciate the nuances of their talk: Frank Churchill is reticent about his knowledge of Jane, until he finds that Jane has been silent on the matter. When he does speak of her, he hesitates, apparently not quite knowing how much knowledge he should claim of her. We notice he is of the opinion that reserved people, like Jane, are silent because they want to be safe. We notice how he finds a way of avoiding Emma's first question about how well he knows Jane, thus giving himself time to think of an answer, and that his answer directs Emma back to Jane herself. When he looks at Mr Elton's house he seems inclined to believe that poverty may be acceptable, if accompanied by love, though Mrs Weston smiles at his romanticism. Behind the artless flow of the dialogue there is a firm structure which is composed of unanswered questions about fact, attitude and relationship. Emma tries to pierce the mist by question and hypothesis, but these questions and guesses are the material out of which the novel is made. Jane Austen's belief about the world appears to be that truth can be found; the same view applies to the fictional world she is creating, but she is not yet ready to reveal it.

Emma's attention is now absorbed by a trifling social circumstance which her snobbery gives a significance it scarcely deserves. She is afraid she is not being invited to a party, which she had not meant to attend, because it was being given by the Coles, a family whose wealth has been made in trade. She is annoyed, however, to find that other families of her own rank have been invited: she will not be able to give them the lesson she thinks they deserve. Now she feels slighted by being left out; the omission may be a tribute to her dignity, but she will miss a pleasant social gathering with her friends. Nevertheless, when the invitation comes she is disposed to relent.

The pleasure Emma takes in the party at the Coles' is because of the further opportunity it gives her for analysis and interpretation (Chapter 25). On arrival, she displays her detective skills by affecting to find in Mr Knightley's manner signs that he has come in his carriage like a gentleman, instead of arriving more modestly on horseback. The next spur to 'that very dear part of Emma, her fancy' comes when she hears of the delivery to Jane Fairfax of a pianoforte from an unknown source, though people suppose that her guardian, Colonel Campbell, has sent it. Seeing a smile on Frank Churchill's face, Emma confides that she not only believes this supposition wrong, but thinks the gift is from Mr Dixon, the husband of her friend, the Colonel's daughter. Emma, of course, has long assumed that Jane had fallen in love with him at Weymouth, though, as she says, 'One might guess twenty things without guessing exactly the right.' Frank Churchill, who has seen Jane with the Dixons, has no knowledge of Jane's attachment but he does not doubt that, if Emma had been there, she would have 'made some discoveries'. He is content to agree that the piano is 'an offering of love'. When Jane is questioned about it later, she blushes and looks as if she wants to say as little about it as possible.

When we begin to examine Emma's reasoning, we discover the part that prejudice plays in her assessment of probabilities. There is nothing much to guide her in tackling the first mild puzzle of the evening: caught in the act of staring at Jane, Frank says he is struck by the odd way she has done her hair. He goes to ask Jane if it is an Irish fashion (Mr Dixon and his wife are, of course, in Ireland), but since he stands between Jane and Emma, the latter cannot see whether Jane blushes. More alarming than puzzling is Mrs Weston's conjecture that Mr Knightley is in love with Jane. Mr Knightley has not used his carriage to assert his social superiority, but to bring Jane and her aunt to the party. Mrs Weston does not accept Emma's view that it is an act of 'simple disinterested benevolence'. Emma determinedly rejects the idea: Mr Knightley must not marry because his nephew is to inherit his estate; he must not marry Jane Fairfax, because her aunt is a tiresome woman; he must not marry because he does not want to and is better off as he is. But Mrs Weston is unimpressed. Mr Knightley has always spoken well of Jane and of her musical talent in particular; why should he not have sent the pianoforte himself? Faced with the fancies of another, Emma is a model of common sense:

> 'You take up an idea, Mrs Weston, and run away with it; as you have many a time reproached me with doing. I see no sign of attachment — I believe nothing of the pianoforté — and proof only shall convince me that Mr Knightley has any thought of marrying Jane Fairfax.' (*Chapter 26*)

It is the first time that Emma has grasped the crucial difference between conjecture and proof.

The musical interlude that follows gives tangible form to the implicit rivalry between Emma and Jane. Emma notices Frank sitting beside Jane and it later appears that he and Jane used to sing together at Weymouth. Frank Churchill has also sung with Emma, who on this occasion has been asked to sing first. But Emma is also concerned about Mr Knightley: 'she could not at all endure the idea of Jane Fairfax at Donwell Abbey.' Questions to Mr Knightley convince her that he has not sent Jane the piano but she cannot be sure that he has no affection for her. As the singing gives way to dancing, Emma can take comfort from the fact that Mr Knightley does not join in. Frank has asked Emma to dance, as she might expect; but it is only the fact that it is growing late that prevents him dancing with Jane. Readers may already have decided the likely outcome of the relationships between the characters, but does this matter? The point of *Emma* does not lie in the reader's finding out about them, but in Emma's failure to do so. The fun of the novel lies in its portrait of a myopic detective, sure of her own investigative ability, but continually taken aback by the mysterious turn of events.

At the beginning of the ninth chapter of Volume Two (Chapter 27), Jane Austen's portrayal of her heroine, musing on her evening at the Coles' is almost frankly comic. When we are told that 'all that she might be supposed to have lost on the side of dignified seclusion, must be amply repaid in the splendour of popularity', the language sounds like Edward Gibbon commenting on the unexpected appearance of a Roman Emperor before his people. Even Emma could scarcely think that in pleasing the Coles she had 'left a name behind her that would not soon die away.' Emma is dimly aware that she has been wrong to reveal her suspicions about Jane Fairfax to Frank Churchill, but she defends herself by saying that the idea was too strong for her to keep to herself and that Frank's deference to her opinion had made her feel she was right. When she compares herself unfavourably with Jane and resolves not to be idle, her repentance lasts for an hour and a half. Her lack of insight into her own conduct is mitigated by the dim sense that it might not be altogether right. It is this teasing, though inadequate, sense of the good which saves Emma from the author's censure and converts to comedy what might be a tasteless muddle.

Now the novel focuses more closely on the relationship between Frank, Emma and Jane. We have become aware that the road from Randalls to Hartfield leads through Highbury, where Miss Bates's house in the High Street overlooks Ford's shop. Found waiting there while Harriet hesitates over a purchase, Emma is persuaded by Miss Bates and Mr Weston to inspect the new pianoforte. Frank has reminded his step-mother of a promise she has made to do so, though she cannot remember it. (We may also notice his remark to Emma, 'I am the wretchedest being in the world about a civil falsehood' (Chaper 27)—an opinion of himself which Emma does not share.) Frank has to be persuaded to join the ladies, the real object of his visit being Hartfield. A closer look at the little episode is revealing: when Emma sees Mrs Weston and Frank, she assumes they are going to Hartfield; Mrs Weston says she is fulfilling her promise to listen to the piano; Frank immediately offers to join Emma and go back with her to Hartfield to wait for his stepmother. Mrs Weston is surprised at his change of plan (as she believes it to be) and asks him to accompany her on her visit to Miss Bates, where he has soon made himself sufficiently at home to replace the rivet in Mrs Bates's spectacles. Embedded in the apparently trivial details of a commonplace scene is substantial evidence that Frank Churchill's behaviour is not straightforward.

As the visit progresses we become more aware of the untrustworthiness of appearances (Chapter 28). Frank's remarks about the origins of the piano are enough to make Jane blush, but the blush occurs also when he mentions the dancing which was cut short at the Coles'. He says he 'would have given worlds—all the worlds one ever has to give—for another half hour.' We remember from the end of Chapter 26 that in another half-hour he would have danced with Jane, and we may think that the only world he has to give is himself. Now Frank teases Jane about where the piano has come from: although he accepts that Colonel Campbell must have sent it, his choice of words hints at another source—'True affection only could have prompted it.' Jane's blush and smile suggests some secret source of happiness, which

Emma thinks 'very reprehensible'. Emma is afraid Frank's tone will upset Jane, but if she has done something wrong, she ought to be ashamed. When Emma supposes she detects some signs of shame, Frank disagrees. Jane is now playing *his* favourite tune, he tells Emma, but there is an ambiguity about the reference of that adjective. A conversation between Miss Bates and Mr Knightley on horseback below her window produces its own drama. The subject of his greeting is Jane; his aim is to do the family service. He is willing to come in when told that Emma and Harriet are there, but the mention of Frank Churchill puts him off. When Miss Bates praises the singing of Frank and Emma, Mr Knightley praises Jane. The whole episode has, of course, been permeated by the extraordinarily disjointed discourses of Miss Bates who can move with celerity from her mother's spectacles to Jane's appetite, from Mr Woodhouse's opinion of baked apples to the gloves she bought the day before, from the merits of Frank Churchill to the generosity of Mr Knightley. Her speech is a medley of all the topics which fall by chance under her attention. However lacking in organisation or logic, Miss Bates's monologues are suffused with an innocent 'candour', a sprightly determination to look on the bright side.

The motif of dancing, first introduced when Frank Churchill looked at the Crown Inn in Chapter 24, burgeons into a proposal for a dance at Randalls. The idea is subjected to careful scrutiny by the Westons on practical grounds and by Mr Woodhouse, on grounds of health. Frank Churchill's interest is so impetuous that Emma begins to be glad she does not intend to marry him. The blend of interest is beautifully done, the urgency of the young man properly subdued by the anxious cares of his elders. It is Miss Bates—that 'standing lesson of how to be happy' (Chapter 29)—who is invited to adjudicate on the suitability of the arrangements.

It is no surprise to Emma—it has been her greatest fear—that Frank's ailing aunt effectively vetoes the dance by recalling him to Enscombe, the big house whose wealth exerts such a powerful influence over those directly connected with it (Chapter 30). Jane Fairfax's unexpectedly open anticipation of pleasure is turned to 'unbecoming indifference'; Mr Knightley's lack of interest changes to a more cheerful regret for his friends' disappointment. Jane Austen focuses on Frank Churchill's leave-taking of Emma. It does not surprise us that he has visited Highbury before coming to Hartfield (Mrs Weston's note to Emma says this is what he means to do), but Emma assumes that he has come to see her first. Frank's regrets at the cancellation of the ball are real enough, but his sadness at leaving Highbury is more difficult to believe in; as Emma points out, his delay in visiting the town did not imply any eagerness to see it. It is when Frank speaks of his visit to Miss Bates that there is a hint off a wish to unburden himself. Emma thinks the awkward silence refers to herself: Jane Austen carefully chooses a broken sentence to indicate the point at which they misunderstand one another. Their consciousness of closeness is acute, but their expectations of one another are ill-founded. He believes she is so generally right that she will be able to guess what he wants to say. Each looks at the other attempting to fathom a hidden intention. Emma interprets Frank's interrupted sentence (which she has repeated almost word for word) as meaning that his visit to Highbury was to bid farewell, but his visit to Hartfield is to propose. That is why she tries to stop him speaking. She even believes his love for her is so strong that she falls in love with him herself.

The force of Jane Austen's method can be seen when Emma transforms her impressions into a retrospective judgment on the scene:

> . . . he had *almost* told her that he loved her. What strength, or what constancy of affection he might be subject to, was another point; but at present she could not doubt his having a decidedly warm admiration, a conscious preference for herself; and this persuasion, joined to all the rest, made her think she *must* be a little in love with him, in spite of every previous determination against it. (*Chapter 30*)

The hesitations, the broken sentences, the doubtful glances of their conversation have been assimilated into a smooth chain of logically connected sentences. She is sure he loves her; his love has caused her to love him in return. Her own lack of concentration, her boredom and frustration, are further signs of the love she has, as it were, caught from him. ('Love' here is spoken of as if it were a disease or an irresistible physical force which has to be obeyed.) Jane Fairfax's 'unbecoming indifference', on the other hand, has merely been a sign of 'the languor of ill-health'. But she decides she must refuse him; their feelings for each other will subside into friendship. A letter to Mrs Weston offers more reasons for thinking him attached to her, but Emma seizes on a reference to Harriet as a means of escape from his affection. Since she believes that men are mainly interested in a pretty face and a sweet temper, she believes that she can divert Frank's love from herself to Harriet. ('Love' is a physical force which can be manipulated at will.)

The disappearance of Frank Churchill signals the introduction of Mrs Elton and an alteration in the balance of the social forces of Highbury. Emma makes it a point of 'pride or propriety' to visit the newly-wedded pair with Harriet (Chapter 32). Now the word 'elegance' is rescued from its simple meaning of mere good taste and restored to its sense of propriety and contrasted with the word 'ease', which suggests something other than the modest demeanour appropriate to a bride. Emma assumes the dominant attitude of an assured upper-class woman; Mrs Elton asserts her rights as the wife of a clergyman with an income of her own. Harriet's 'tenderness of heart' makes her incapable of Emma's critical survey of Mrs Elton's person and pretension. In Emma's view,

Mrs Elton was a vain woman, extremely well satisfied with herself, and thinking much of her own importance; that she meant to shine and be very superior, but with manners which had been formed in a bad school, pert and familiar; that all her notions were drawn from one set of people, and one style of living; that if not foolish she was ignorant, and that her society would certainly do Mr Elton no good. (*Chapter 32*)

The judgment is concise and assured: much of it is borne out in practice, but some of these terms might easily apply to Emma herself, and there is certainly a tacit acknowledgement that Mrs Elton may be a threat to her own social superiority.

Mrs Elton's strategy is soon revealed: she has her own standards against which Hartfield—'so extremely like Maple Grove' (Chapter 32) (her brother's house in suburbia)—may be judged. She has no doubt about the superiority of the county to which she has come and which she intends to explore in her brother's barouche-landau, a new acquisition she finds frequent occasion to mention. Her observations on Mr Woodhouse's health, on Emma's single state, and the benefits her friendship might confer are as intolerable as they are impertinent. Her references to her life in Bath are ominous signals of superficiality. When she speaks of music of which she professes to be 'passionately fond', she gushes and contradicts herself. The poor impression she makes reaches a climax in her praise of Mrs Weston as 'quite the gentlewoman' (despite her previous occupation). Emma's response states some key terms for what counts as good behaviour:

'Mrs Weston's manners', said Emma, 'were always particularly good. Their propriety, simplicity, and elegance would make them the safest model for any young woman.' (*Chapter 32*)

But Mrs Elton is unabashed, quite equal to discovering 'that Mr Knightley is a gentleman.' Emma's exclamatory commentary underlines the features of language which express Mrs Elton's vulgarity: her 'Knightley', 'Mr E.' and '*caro sposo*' suggest a slapdash familiarity far from the restraint of elegance and propriety. She is over-emphatic, self-conscious and self-dramatising: there is something suspect about her talk of the 'sacrifice' she has made in coming to Highbury, of the 'retirement' of her future home, of the 'resources' she has within her, and of the 'world' she is prepared to give up for Mr Elton. The language of romantic fiction is scarcely appropriate to the wife of the vicar of Highbury.

On this occasion Emma's judgment is assimilated into the narrative commentary. She considers Mrs Elton 'self-important, presuming, familiar, and ill-bred.' The sentence, 'Her observation had been pretty correct', is carried within the style of free indirect speech, but it is not suggested that Emma's opinion on this occasion is misguided, even if it is not shared by her neighbours who are 'disposed to commend, or not in the habit of judging.'

Before relations between the two cool, however, Mrs Elton makes it clear how much she thinks of Jane Fairfax: here is someone she can treat as an interesting inferior, whom she can entertain and whose horizons she can widen, in what is almost a parody of Emma's relationship with Harriet. To Emma's surprise, Jane is willing to accept Mrs Elton's company, though she has refused a second invitation to join the Campbells in Ireland. Mrs Weston thinks Jane is glad of some respite from Miss Bates, while Mr Knightley suggests she has failed to find a friend in Emma herself. Mrs Elton, he suggests, will find it impossible to patronise Jane as she would like; she will soon feel the force of Jane's superiority. These remarks lead Emma to confront him about his feelings for Jane: the Coles have been publicly speculating about a link between them. Mr Knightley is quick to rebut the idea, and Emma draws back from the suggestion that she has been planning a match for him. His criticism of Jane's lack of openness echoes her own.

The last three chapters of the second volume of the novel consist of a leisurely account of the dinner-party Emma gives for the Eltons: Harriet, of course, begs to be excused and Jane goes in her place. The careful balance of the evening—always so necessary for Mr Woodhouse's equanimity—is upset by the unexpected arrival of John Knightley and his two sons. It is they who have spotted Jane Fairfax walking through the rain to the post-office, a topic which leads to speculation about Jane's future and to Mrs Elton's officious assertion of a right to decide how she should collect her mail. For the first time we see Jane at close quarters. There is a sadness, verging on tears, when John Knightley speaks of her future, which he implies will include marriage and children. There is a determination, quiet but resolute, not to be governed by Mrs Elton. Letters, post-offices and handwriting—Emma defends Frank Churchill's handwriting against Mrs Knightley's charge of unmanliness—are too prominent subjects of conversation not to be significant later, though their significance is not revealed here. In the drawing-room Mrs Elton maintains her assault on Jane Fairfax, urging her to accept her help in finding a teaching post. Jane's feelings about becoming a governess are candidly expressed: in comparison to the slave-trade it is

> . . . widely different certainly as to the guilt of those who carry it on; but as to the greater misery of the victims, I do not know where it lies. (*Chapter 35*)

To a modern ear Jane's talk of the sale 'not quite of human flesh—but of human intellect' (Chapter 35) has a suggestion of prostitution rather than of slavery; what cannot be missed is her detestation of a profession which would put her in the hands of a family approved of by Mrs Elton, who is obliged to consider whether even Jane's talents would permit her to be treated as an equal. Despite Jane's firm wish not to be indebted to her, Mrs Elton's desire to manage her life is irrepressible.

When Mr Weston joins them from London, he brings news of Frank's imminent arrival. The narrative records Emma's excitement, but it does not fail to mention Jane Fairfax, who is, however, too deep in conversation to be told directly.

The volume ends on a quieter note: Emma defends herself from Mr John Knightley's strictures about the dissipations of her social life. His brother suggests Randalls is the source of new excitement, but he means Frank Churchill, not the Westons. The point at issue is who is best fitted to look after Mr John Knightley's two boys: when Emma says that 'aunt Emma' is as able as 'uncle Knightley', she brings Mr Knightley and herself together as part of an established relationship which we may feel (even if the protagonists do not) has still to be explored. It is another example of that unspoken trust in each other which we have noticed before as one of the assumptions of the narrative.

## Volume Three (*Chapters 37–55*)

The third volume of the novel consists of a series of episodes which subject Emma's composure and self-assurance, her clear-sightedness and integrity to the severest test. Now Mr Knightley plays a more active role as Emma's sternest critic and as a primary source of value. Though Emma thinks Frank Churchill is in love with her, she finds he is less so than she fears. The reader knows how often his thoughts turn to Highbury, but Emma interprets his restlessness as a fear of his feelings for her. Now his relationship with Highbury enters a period of obscurity. Although his ailing aunt has moved from Yorkshire to London, and then to Richmond—a mere nine miles away—Frank does not seem to see his friends as often as we might expect. The previously postponed ball takes place at the Crown Inn and Mrs Elton signifies her approval, but Frank is strangely restless. He has appeared to be impatient to meet her, but perhaps he was only impatient to meet Jane whom Mrs Elton has characteristically forgotten to call for with her carriage. When he backs away from Mrs Elton's effusive compliments (she obviously expects that he will dance with her), Emma takes him to task for being ungrateful. His smiling response holds a question for the reader: is he ungrateful for Mrs Elton's compliments, as Emma seems to imply, or because she has sent her carriage back for Jane, as Frank may think she does. When the question of Mrs Elton's right to begin the ball is raised, Frank claims Emma as his partner. When Mr Elton tries to snub Harriet, Mr Knightley rescues her by asking her to dance with him (it has already occurred to Emma that he is too young and handsome not to be dancing with the rest). Mr Knightley is shrewd enough to guess that the Eltons dislike Emma because she meant Elton to marry Harriet; he does not know that Elton had designs on Emma herself. Emma is quick to show her gratitude to Mr Knightley: their conversation is touched by tenderness, as she confesses her fault in thinking well of Mr Elton, and he praises her serious spirit which saves her when her vanity leads her astray. This is the first explicit recognition of the blend of seriousness and silliness of which Emma's character is composed, and which is an essential feature of the novel's theme and even of its structure. Once more the closeness of their existing friendship is referred to, and Jane Austen once more uses the relationship between brother and sister as an analogue for the bond between husband and wife. Notice in the following quotation how Emma suggests the first relationship and Knightley, by rejecting it, almost implies the other:

> 'Whom are you going to dance with?' asked Mr Knightley.
> She hesitated a moment, and then replied, 'With you, if you will ask me.'
> 'Will you?' said he, offering his hand.
> 'Indeed I will. You have shown that you can dance, and you know we are not really so much brother and sister as to make it at all improper.'
> 'Brother and sister! no, indeed.' (*Chapter 38*)

Of course, it is perfectly true that Emma is saying it would not be proper for brother and sister to dance together. (We may remember in *Northanger Abbey* how Henry Tilney compares dancing to marriage.) But she is saying that she feels almost as close to Knightley as to a brother, just as he is saying that his feelings towards her are more than brotherly. The slow approach of hero and heroine to a recognition of the intimacy they already share is but one more example of the subtlety of this novel, as it traces the link between true self-knowledge and a reliable knowledge of others.

The unexpected encounter between Harriet and the gypsies (in Chapter 39) and her rescue by Frank Churchill offer Emma a new cue for matchmaking. The reader notices Frank's continued connection with his friends at Highbury, but Emma supposes Frank and Harriet have been brought closer by their adventure. As the narrator drily comments,

> Could a linguist, could a grammarian, could even a mathematician have seen what she did, have witnessed their appearance together, and heard their history of it, without feeling that circumstances have been at work to make them peculiarly interesting to each other?—How much more must an imaginist, like herself, be on fire with speculation and foresight! —especially with such a ground-work of anticipation as her mind had already made. (*Chapter 39*)

We cannot assume that the last of these sentences is spoken, or thought, by Emma, though the first is surely an ironical report of what she might have said to herself. The word 'imaginist', placed alongside 'linguist' and 'mathematician' ironically suggests that Emma's speculation has the authority of scholarship. Her 'ground-work of anticipation' includes knowing that Harriet is recovering from her obsession with Mr Elton, and believing that Frank Churchill is trying to overcome his passion for herself. Principles of simplicity, coherence and resemblance are more significant to her thought-processes than any matter of fact.

That Harriet's thoughts are turning to Frank appear to be borne out by her destroying 'treasures' she associates with Elton and by her admission that she loves someone socially superior to herself. The episodes that Harriet refers to, involving Mr Elton's sticking plaster and his borrowed pencil, are quite new, but Jane Austen links them plausibly to moments in the fictional past. We notice that Emma merely assumes that Harriet is in love with Frank, since she is now too cautious to mention a name. Both refer to a service this new lover has done for Harriet in the past, but perhaps only the very observant reader will remember that being saved from the gypsies is not the only service Harriet has had done for her in the recent past.

It is Mr Knightley who now brings a critical eye to the 'schemes and hopes and connivance' (Chapter 41) which have largely been the products of Emma's fantasy. While Frank Churchill is generally thought to be interested in Emma, and Emma supposes he is interested in Harriet, Knightley's observations of some looks which have been exchanged lead him to think that Frank is interested in Jane. More significant is the fact that some information known to Frank — and to Miss Bates — does not appear to have come from Mrs Weston. When Frank plays word-games afterwards at Hartfield, it is the word 'blunder' which he offers to Jane, whose blush suggests some complicity between them. It is an association which troubles Mr Knightley, who has long mistrusted Frank Churchill: now his mistrust seems to spread to Jane Fairfax. Frank's childish game which conceals 'gallantry and trick' reminds us of the deep moral considerations which are hidden beneath the surface of this novel: manners are connected with morals; overt behaviour is not the whole of behaviour — it is linked to the hidden aims, purposes and attitudes to which praise or blame may be attached, a consideration which applies with as much force to Miss Bates as to Frank or Emma. A spirit of mischief prompts Frank to present Emma with the word 'Dixon'; when he shows it to Jane, she reacts with a blush of displeasure. Mr Knightley is puzzled: there is some shared secret between Emma and Frank, but he also believes some odd intimacy exists between Frank and Jane Fairfax. When he confides his belief to Emma, she assures him there is nothing between Frank and Jane.

External events now make their effect on this haze of possibilities. Mrs Elton's sister does not pay her expected visit, thus depriving her of the barouche-landau; a projected outing has to be postponed because a horse is lame. When Mrs Elton finds the resources she has boasted of cannot support the consequent boredom, a visit is arranged to Donwell Abbey. Mrs Elton finds in it an excuse for playing at rural simplicity, but Mr Knightley prefers to manage the expedition according to his standards rather than hers. He follows the example Mr Weston has set in inviting both Emma's and

Mrs Elton's set of friends. And Mr Weston with unbounded good nature undertakes to invite Frank Churchill. The events of the afternoon are desultory and disconnected: Mrs Elton's enthusiasm for strawberry-picking is soon overcome by the heat; Emma is glad to look at the grounds of the Abbey with the eye of a close associate of its proprietor; Mr Knightley talks to Harriet, as they both look down on Robert Martin's farm; Mrs Elton is more insistent on finding Jane a job than Jane's patience can bear; Frank Churchill does not come. The unbecoming climax of these events is the agitated departure of Jane Fairfax, seen only by Emma, whom she asks to tell the others she is going. Emma puts her distress down to the privations of her home life, but they hardly seem to explain her vehemently expressed wish to be alone. When Frank Churchill arrives a little later, he is out of temper. He has met Jane on the way; something has made him even more mercurial than usual; he talks of going abroad when his aunt is better. When Emma invites him to join their expedition to Box Hill the next day, he first refuses, then is persuaded to stay.

The expedition to Box Hill is one of the most significant episodes in the novel. The apparent unity of the previous day has broken up; the company has formed into smaller groups: the Eltons keep to themselves, Harriet and Emma are with Frank, Mr Knightley looks after Jane and Miss Bates. Emma and Frank become the animated centre of a dull company. Frank's flirtatious banter almost embarrasses Emma, but worse is to come when he tries to rouse the others by bidding them, in Emma's name, say one thing clever, two things moderately clever or three things 'very dull indeed' (Chapter 43). When Miss Bates rises to the bait, Emma cuttingly wonders how she will be able to confine herself to three.

Emma has caused pain, which Mr Weston tries to cover up by a clumsy play on Emma's name. Mr and Mrs Elton walk off rather than submit to playing a game for Emma's benefit. The mood alters when Frank Churchill embarks on some remarks on marriage — how difficult it is to know a woman merely on a casual acquaintance in a public place:

> It is only by seeing women in their own homes, among their own set, just as they always are, that you can form any just judgment. Short of that, it is all guess and luck — and will generally be ill-luck. How many a man has committed himself on a short acquaintance, and rued it all the rest of his life! (*Chapter 43*)

This draws from Jane Fairfax one of her rare speeches of any length whose point lies in a stinging reference to

> . . . weak, irresolute characters (whose happiness must always be at the mercy of chance), who will suffer an unfortunate acquaintance to be an inconvenience, an oppression for ever. (*Chapter 43*)

When Frank Churchill asks Emma to choose a wife for him, she thinks of Harriet. But Jane decides it is time to join Mrs Elton.

With the help of Mr Knightley's sharp observation, the reader is now alert to what the narrative is leaving unreported. Frank Churchill's vacillations and Jane's volatile behaviour can now be understood. Jane would not willingly seek out the company of Mrs Elton: some strong aversive forces must be pushing her into the arms of a woman anxious to see her placed in a menial position which she detests. Beneath the surface triviality of the events we have been witnessing lies a tale of suffering and passionate feeling, which gradually takes shape out of the fog of speculation and misunderstanding, self-advertisement and triviality generated by Mrs Elton and the weaker side of Emma herself.

Before the wretched day ends, Mr Knightley draws Emma aside to point out the heartlessness of her conduct to Miss Bates. In his eyes Emma's complaints about Miss Bates's absurdity do not excuse her:

> 'It was badly done, indeed! — You, whom she had known from an infant, whom she had seen grow up from a period when her notice was on honour, to have you now, in thoughtless spirits, and the pride of the moment, laugh at her, humble her — and before her niece too . . . '
> (*Chapter 43*)

The dimension of time, in which the moment counts for nothing unless it is part of an ordered pattern, humbles human pride and reminds us of the relentless transformations to which all are subject. What Emma fails to see about Miss Bates are those simple facts about being human which ought to prompt her to see resemblance rather than difference. Despite Mr Weston's flattering suggestion that her name expresses perfection, Emma is not perfect, and, perhaps for the first time, she feels the truth of it. Now her feelings are 'only of anger against herself, mortification and deep concern'. It is a significant moment in the novel when Emma sees not with the eye of fantasy but of truth, and what she sees coincides with the view of a man who has been patiently faithful to her true interests. As we learned on first meeting him, he 'was one of the few people who could see faults in Emma Woodhouse, and the only one who ever told her of them.' Now he has offered her a verbal picture of herself, representing features of her character which no physical sketch could convey.

Emma tries to put her remorseful feelings to practical use by spending the evening with her father and by going early next day to visit Miss Bates. She is not able to see Jane who has taken to bed feeling ill. After hearing that Frank Churchill had returned to Richmond, she had settled with Mrs Elton to accept a post with one of her friends. Jane declines to see Emma, though it seems she would have consented to see 'Mrs Cole or any other steady friend'. Emma has to accept the implied rebuke to her reliability, just as she must wince when Miss Bates describes her as 'always kind'. It is her mistrust of Frank's intentions, presumably, as much as Mrs Elton's pertinacity, which has forced Jane to accept a post she has always dreaded.

Emma's kindness to Miss Bates at least has the effect of pleasing Mr Knightley whose impulse is to kiss her hand. Once again, there passes between them a wonderfully described moment of mutual esteem:

> It seemed as if there were an instantaneous impression in her favour, as if his eyes received the truth from her's, and all that had passed of good in her feelings were at once caught and honoured. (*Chapter 45*)

Now, in their silent conversation there is no fantasy, no supposition; her eyes convey truth and he sees that the truth reveals goodness. Does this glance of mutual esteem imply something about Jane Austen's beliefs — namely, that there is a connection between the objectivity of truth and the objectivity of moral goodness? Emma cannot be sure whether she offered him the hand he took; she knew he meant to kiss it, though he failed to do so, but

> She could not but recall the attempt with great satisfaction. It spoke such perfect amity. (*Chapter 45*)

It is of such moments of the interaction of body and spirit that Jane Austen appears to believe love is made: she describes their extraordinary fleeting intangibility with rare tenderness.

Mrs Churchill's death is the catalyst which precipitates the rest of the action of the novel. Now Emma learns from Mrs Weston that Frank has been secretly engaged to Jane Fairfax for eight or nine months. Although Emma can truly assert that she is not affected, the Westons are clearly unhappy about Frank's behaviour. Emma has things to regret in her insinuations about Jane and her hopes for Harriet: she is perfectly clear about what has been wrong with Frank's behaviour:

> What right had he to come along with affection and faith engaged, and with manners so *very* disengaged? (*Chapter 46*)

In this matter which concerns herself, Emma sees very closely what is right. Frank Churchill is

> So unlike what a man should be! — None of that upright integrity, that strict adherence to truth and principle, that disdain of trick and littleness, which a man should display in every transaction of his life. (*Chapter 46*)

It is a further clarification of what should be permanent and real from one not noted for steady adherence to public standards of objectivity and truth. Emma seems to have discovered a use for the language of objective morality. Some things are wrong, despite what people may think of them; it is possible to conceive of a man who would exemplify values she cares about; we may indeed believe we know the man she is describing, especially since her phrase 'trick and littleness' carries echoes of the phrase 'gallantry and trick' which Knightley has earlier used of Frank Churchill. Now Emma is able to imagine (in the true sense of the word) the recent sufferings of Jane Fairfax. Part of her anger at being deceived arises from the uncharitable indiscretions it has tempted her to. But she is able to congratulate Mr Weston on his son's choice of a girl whose 'steadiness of character and good judgment' have served her well in trying circumstances.

Having revealed the major secret of the novel, Jane Austen is left only with what remains for Emma to discover about herself. For a second time Emma has seen her plans for Harriet collapse in ruins. The close reporting of Emma's thoughts and feelings give the reader a living sense of the guilt and anger which agitate her. She has encouraged Harriet to think of Frank, and a second disappointment is likely to be severe. When Emma and Harriet meet, Jane Austen reverts to dramatising the scene, refusing us privileged knowledge of her characters' thoughts and feelings. Harriet and Emma have credited one another with too close an understanding. Now a succession of blushes, agitated voices, opposed body postures, averted faces, and broken eye-contact accompanies Harriet's explanation, halting at first but growing in self-confidence and resolution, that it is Mr Knightley whom she loves and who, she believes, loves her in return. It is now clear how much she has benefited from Emma's lessons in elegance: Mr Knightley is infinitely more gentlemanly than Frank Churchill, and Harriet's belief that he has shown an interest in her is made with a dignified simplicity which does her credit.

In sending us back to the closed world of Emma's inner consciousness, Jane Austen employs a style of writing which is more direct than the free indirect speech hitherto used to report her states of mind. Now we are given the very words, exclamations and questions which go through her mind, as well as a direct account of her thought processes. The speed as well as the certain aim of her thinking is suggested by the metaphor Jane Austen uses:

. . . it darted through her, with the speed of an arrow, that Mr Knightley must marry no one but herself. (*Chapter 47*)

In this crisis, and despite the agitation of her feelings, she remains outwardly calm. She knows it is in her own interest to pay attention to what Harriet has said, since it would be a misplaced superiority to pity her, if she was right in thinking that Mr Knightley loved her.

Harriet's case rests on a summary of the treatment she has received from Knightley since the momentous occasion when he danced with her at the Crown Inn. On other occasions he had been kind to her, had praised her gentleness and asked if there was anyone she was fond of. Here Jane Austen gives some details, not reported at the time, of Harriet's conversation with Mr Knightley on the day of the trip to Donwell Abbey at a spot overlooking Abbey Mill Farm when Robert Martin's name was in Harriet's thoughts, even if only to be dismissed. When Emma now makes the connection explicit, suggesting that Mr Knightley had meant her to think again about the farmer, Harriet's rejection of the idea is emphatic. Once again, she makes it clear how well Emma's lesson has been learnt: only the best will now be good enough for her.

Jane Austen does not disguise the impatient anger Emma feels toward Harriet. Again we are plunged into the turmoil of her thoughts, unprotected by any indirect presentation. We are shown the urgent questions about her own conduct that flood through her mind; we are told of the mental comparisons she makes between Knightley and Frank Churchill and the clear conclusions she draws from them. The result is Emma's most explicit condemnation of her own past folly: she has been arrogant, vain, mistaken and mischievous. If Harriet is right, the event which she fears will have been brought about by herself. Now, when Harriet seeks to rise in the social scale and lay claim to someone Emma wants for herself, she is clear about Harriet's real worth and legitimate claim. Emma's clear-sightedness, we may think, has its origin in a sharper sense of her own self-interest. Her new stance does not make her more just to Harriet, but it is grounded upon something deeper than a need to look well in the eyes of others.

As she focuses on the debates Emma has with herself, Jane Austen allows the cooler voice of the narrator to take over from Emma's own disjointed exclamations. Even if her tone is still to be heard in the account of her past relationships with Knightley, the account is dispassionate and objective. She has always depended on being 'first in interest and affection' with him, but she 'could not flatter herself with any idea of blindness in his attachment to *her*' (Chapter 48). Emma has always believed that romantic love, as experienced by men, had an element that was wholly irrational: on this force depended her expectation that Mr Elton and Frank Churchill would be sufficiently attracted by Harriet to ignore her defects of intelligence and social position. Holding this belief, she cannot rule out the possibility that Mr Knightley has succumbed to a pretty face. If only she had chosen to befriend Jane Fairfax instead of Harriet Smith, this situation would not have arisen, and she would not have found herself in the position of suggesting that Jane had improper feelings for the husband of her best friend. Just as Emma has no reason to congratulate herself on her treatment of Jane, so Jane has experienced nothing but misery in her ill-judged clandestine engagement to Frank Churchill. The value of open, principled, straightforward behaviour is clear. For Emma the future appears gloomy with the prospect of a declining circle of friends and the possible loss of Mr Knightley; her only hope lies 'in the resolution of her own better conduct' and in being 'more rational, more acquainted with herself.'

The melancholy of this time has been accompanied by 'cold stormy rain', but the next day it clears and 'it was summer again' (Chapter 49). There is a parallel improvement in Emma's fortunes: Mr Knightley returns from London, and a final scene of comic misunderstanding about what each is feeling is played out. He thinks she is in love with Frank; she thinks the confidences she tries to prevent him making are connected with Harriet. But comedy gives way to sentiment. Emma explains that Frank Churchill's attentions made her believe—but only for a moment—that she was in love with him. Now she can see that his behaviour was part of 'a deeper game', as Mr Knightley put it on an earlier occasion. Frank has used her to mask a relationship with Jane which it was prudent to conceal while Mrs Churchill was alive. Now Knightley has the opportunity to envy the lovers' happiness, to declare himself in favour of marriage, and to express his own feelings for Emma. Jane Austen's strategy of concealment, of concentrating almost exclusively on Emma's flawed insight into her companions may be thought to have worked to the disadvantage of Knightley, who has had few opportunities to play the romantic hero. Emma has taken him too much for granted for us to know him well. In this scene Jane Austen works hard to rehabilitate him, using his silence to indicate depth of feeling and a keen sensitivity to the possibility of rejection.

This presentation of Knightley's proposal is deliberately low-keyed, but it continues the theme of mutual misunderstanding, showing, however, how imperfect knowledge may be corrected by a responsible willingness to pay attention to others. Emma fears that Knightley is about to tell her about his feelings for Harriet; she wants to change the subject; she appears to him not to want to listen to what he wants to say; he falls silent. It is only when Emma has the courage to put his welfare before her own, by listening to him 'cost her what it would', that she hears him telling her that he loves her. Now the thoughts that go through her mind have a clear grasp of fact and feeling; there is a steadiness, depth and discretion about her view of Harriet and herself and their relationship with Knightley which suggests the measure of her conversion to common sense, to clear-sightedness, to honest feeling and sound judgment. One of the principal themes of the novel has been the difficulty of truthfulness, and of the complex connection between honesty in speech, behaviour and feeling although, as the narrator suggests, there is something fundamental about the dimension of feeling:

> Seldom, very seldom, does complete truth belong to any human disclosure; seldom can it happen that something is not a little disguised, or a little mistaken; but where, as in this case, though the conduct is mistaken, the feelings are not, it may not be very material. (*Chapter 49*)

By a series of happy chances Emma and George Knightley have reached an understanding. Knightley's own story of the discomfort and distress which the relationship between Frank and Emma had caused him is briefly told, as are the rapid and unexpected stages by which these feelings are reversed.

In the last six chapters of the novel the remaining mysteries are cleared up and the remaining awkwardnesses resolved with scrupulous care. Emma's first concern is for her father, her next for Harriet. Mr Woodhouse is one of the least prepossessing characters in the novel; his care for others is rendered useless by the groundless fears from which it springs; he is deeply selfish, and wholly unimaginative; but his foibles, which are tiresome but harmless, make him wholly predictable and therefore a source of comedy. He is also the principal and unquestioned object of Emma's affection, a test of her capacity for disinterested love. Her concern for him is totally unselfconscious, never a source of self-congratulation. Emma decides that she will not marry during his lifetime. Harriet is to be written to, and encouraged to visit London, so that some time may elapse before they meet again.

It is characteristic of Jane Austen's way of constructing her novels that she should now make plain what she has kept hidden, using a letter from Frank Churchill to do so. It contains a vindication of Jane Fairfax: it had required his importunity 'to induce the most upright female mind in the creation to stoop to a secret engagement' (Chapter 50). It apologises for his behaviour towards Emma, offering as defence the excuse that he believes she knew he was not serious, and that she suspected what his feelings were for Jane. Not for the first time Emma is credited with greater perspicacity than she possesses; indeed, the disparity between her public reputation for clear-headedness and her private confusion has been a main source of comedy in the novel. The mystery of the pianoforte is finally solved, and a full account is given of what led to the coldness between Frank and Jane on the outings to Donwell and Box Hill and to Jane's decision to accept the post Mrs Elton had been pressing on her. Some readers may think that such explanations are unnecessary, but Jane Austen is a scrupulous story-teller. She displays in this novel a passion for coherence; she seems determined to show that to the instructed eye there are no mysteries; the density of human motive and human relationship *does* yield to patient, rational scrutiny. The tone of Frank's letter is not without faults: it is impetuous, self-willed, more than a little self-congratulatory. But when he speaks of the suffering he has caused Jane, he is genuinely remorseful; his references to his father, to Mrs Weston and to Emma are as generous as one would expect from a loving son and friend.

Frank's faults do not escape the censure of Mr Knightley whose commentary on the letter appears in the following chapter, but even he is prepared to agree that Frank's defects of character are likely to be offset by Jane's 'steadiness and delicacy of principle' (Chapter 51). Mr Knightley proposes to solve the problem of Mr Woodhouse by living at Hartfield himself. A chapter is devoted to a reconciliation with Jane, which amounts to a greeting and a farewell interrupted by the archness of Mrs Elton, smug in the knowledge of Jane's 'secret' and the flustered incoherence of Miss Bates, who does not quite know how much Emma knows, both ladies finely confusing Frank Churchill and Mr Perry as the cause of Jane's recovery. From Jane there is an apology for the artificial coldness of her previous behaviour; from Emma, a straightforward delight in Jane's prospects of happiness which ends with her sincere gratitude that there are no more secrets between them.

*Emma* is surely a wiser, less rigid novel than *Mansfield Park*. The continuum of good and evil is more insisted upon, the difficulty of separating them more clearly recognised. Even Mr Knightley, sometimes mistakenly seen as an inhuman pattern of virtue, says:

> I am losing all my bitterness against spoilt children, my dearest Emma. I, who am owning all my happiness to *you*, would it not be horrible ingratitude in me to be severe on them? (*Chapter 53*)

Children must be taught principles of behaviour, and it is well for them to have natural gifts; but given these, they may, perhaps, be left to develop without too much interference. When Emma discusses with Knightley the education of Mrs Weston's baby daughter, what seems to matter most is the loving attention which children receive, and the 'disposition to hope for good' which Frank Churchill believes he has inherited from his father. *Emma* is a celebration of the most positive aspects of family life: even John Knightley and his wife have a domestic happiness that George Knightley can envy and profit from by example.

*Emma* ends in happiness: there is almost a superfluity of smiles and laughter. The penultimate chapter begins with intimations of sadness, associated with the return of Harriet Smith from London, which threatens to upset the harmony Emma has achieved. But things turn out otherwise: Emma can scarcely conceal her amazed delight when Mr Knightley tells her that Harriet and Robert Martin, who have come together in the unlikely domestic setting of Mr and Mrs John Knightley, have become engaged. Harriet's case provides the last quiver of misunderstanding between Emma and Knightley: *he* expects Emma to be displeased at Harriet's choice, *she* cannot believe that she should really have accepted Robert Martin, having so recently been adamant about Mr Knightley's superiority. When everything is explained, Mr Knightley is able to praise Harriet for being

> ' . . . an artless, amiable girl, with very good notions, very seriously good principles, and placing her happiness in the affections and utility of domestic life.' (*Chapter 54*)

Generously, but wrongly, he credits Emma with fostering these virtues. Emma and the reader know how mistaken he is, but nothing is said to contradict him. Now that nearly the last tangle has been removed from her life, Emma looks forward to

> Nothing, but to grow more worthy of him, whose intention and judgment had been ever so superior to her own. Nothing, but that the lessons of her past folly might teach her humility and circumspection in the future.

In the final meeting between Jane and Frank and Emma, Jane Austen confronts the dangers of wit and humour. Even while he expresses shame at the harm his duplicity might have caused, Frank cannot help being amused by the memory of what has happened. Emma confesses that she too might have been amused in the same situation; she suggests they are both fortunate in being connected 'with two characters so much superior to our own.' Wit, liveliness and cleverness are morally dangerous characteristics in Jane Austen's fiction; they are likely to be associated with a critical energy which subverts a natural moral order, which requires a submission to virtue and goodness. In this novel each of the flawed central characters is happily attracted to characters of integrity and virtue whose superior qualities will redeem them from fantasy and mischief. The final chapter brings about the marriage of Harriet and Robert Martin—another, if slightly different, example of the matching of weakness with strength. Readers will have to decide for themselves how successful Jane Austen has been in this latest attempt to marry anarchy and order, solid good sense and subversive wit, truth and fantasy, feeling and rationality. At least in this novel, dangerous qualities are tractable, and self-correcting. In contrast to the severity of *Mansfield Park*, *Emma* appears to be a work of a larger and more generous charity to aspects of human nature which cannot easily be kept apart.

# Chapter 7

# *Persuasion*:
# the proper satisfactions
# of the self

## Introduction

If *Emma* is the most carefully planned of Jane Austen's novels, its successor is more succinct, graver, less concerned with the ebb-and-flow of social life, much more concentrated upon the silent suffering of an individual. *Persuasion* is principally concerned with examining the effects of the suppression of feeling in obedience to a sense of duty which it may have been right to obey but whose precepts in the event were wrong. In this novel Jane Austen looks at the source of right conduct and considers in particular what happens when there appears to be a clash between what one ought to do and what one wants to do. What is the place of feeling in moral behaviour?

## Commentary

### Volume One (*Chapters 1–12*)

The opening chapters of *Persuasion* show Jane Austen's style at its most succinct: her judgments of Sir Walter Elliot's vanity are memorable for their exact and pointed brevity. Jane Austen has this character accurately in her sights; she picks him off with words which are too direct for irony; they crackle with the charge of the narrator's tightly-controlled contempt. It is perhaps particularly cruel of Jane Austen to compare him with the complacent valet of a 'new made lord' (Chapter 1) since it is precisely the antiquity of his own title that delights him. Sir Walter's admiration for his own person is matched by his devotion to the established order of society. His attendance, later in the novel, upon the Dowager Viscountess Dalrymple, displays a propensity for fawning on his superiors which is as great as his habit of contempt for those beneath him. Apart from his eldest daughter, Elizabeth, who shares his social attitudes, and Mrs Clay, the daughter of his lawyer, who knows how to please, few others meet his standards. Sir Walter worships a simplified and idealised form of himself — the Sir Walter who has united the gifts of 'beauty' and 'baronetcy'. The self-loving Sir Walter admires selected aspects of himself, which he takes for the whole: this is a classic route to the self-deception and the suppression of inconvenient facts and feelings, which is a central unifying theme of the novel.

Swiftly, we are introduced to the other members of the Elliot family — to Elizabeth, Anne and Mary, Sir Walter's daughters, of whom only Elizabeth matters to their father, though Mary has acquired importance by her marriage to a local landowner, Charles Musgrove, whose sisters, Henrietta and Louisa, are to play a considerable part in the novel. Anne is valued only by her late mother's friend, Lady Russell, to whom some of the responsibility of advising the girls has passed. When the novel opens, Anne is twenty-seven: she is faded and thin with little hope of marriage. Elizabeth is anxious to marry and had hoped to marry her cousin, William Elliot, heir to the baronetcy, but he married someone else and contact with him was lost. Now he is a widower, but he appears to have no wish to renew acquaintance with his uncle. Sir Walter is now in debt: much against his inclination, he is advised to curtail his expenses.

To Anne the issue is simple: Sir Walter has contracted debts which he must pay. He should act like a man of principle and pay them. This scheme is too rigorous for her father who says he would rather leave Kellynch Hall, an idea seized on by his lawyer, Mr Shepherd. The house will be let; the family will move to Bath. This latter suggestion is urged against Anne's advice by Lady Russell, who is presented as a good, loving, dutiful, well-bred and, generally, sensible woman, who shares Sir Walter's sense of the value of an ordered society and the deference due to rank. She is a worthy but limited woman whose place in the novel's moral scheme is ambiguous.

Very skilfully, Jane Austen suggests the persuasiveness with which Lady Russell urges her schemes. On the one hand, her suggestions are naive and artless: they come from a warm, well-disposed heart. On the other, they are facile, prejudiced projections of her sense of what would be fitting for herself. There is a faint echo of Emma Woodhouse in Lady Russell's behaviour: she is equally active in the affairs of others, but what she persuades them to do is not the result of clear-headed analysis. It may well be the contention of the novel, however, that no plan for the future of others can be of this nature. The novel suggests that human action springs from feeling, to defer to the persuasions of others in the belief that they know better is unsound, because a necessary condition of right action is that it be based on the genuine feelings of the agent.

Such larger questions arise from a consideration of the novel as a whole. In the discussion that follows about letting Kellynch Hall, the snobbery and self-regard of Sir Walter are made plain: there is, for example, his fear that public knowledge of his intention to let might damage his reputation. There follows his suggestion that sailors, even if the wealth they have gained in war makes them likely tenants, are unlikely to have experienced the grandeur

Kellynch Hall provides. Mr Shepherd's judicious flattery that what Sir Walter intends is of too much public interest to be long concealed is followed by Anne's less cautious praise of the Navy. Naval officers are as deserving as 'any other set of men' (Chapter 3) because they have worked hard. It is a remark which suggests that merit cuts across established social hierarchy; if baronets are a set of men like any other, their superiority is denied. Sir Walter attacks the Navy on precisely this ground: people of no family are able to get on in the world. Mr Shepherd's vigilance soon produces a tenant too eligible to be passed over. Admiral Croft's gentlemanliness, wealth, and sense of the honour that the tenancy would confer on him, combine with his wife's ability as a manager to recommend them. Mrs Croft's brother-in-law has been—not a gentleman indeed—but the curate of a neighbouring parish. The relationship turns out to be a crucial link with Anne Elliot's mismanaged past.

A second brother of Mrs Croft, Captain Frederick Wentworth, had been in Somersetshire nearly eight years before; he had fallen in love with Anne Elliot and proposed to her. The young man had nothing to recommend him except energy, intelligence and high spirits. His confidence in his own abilities suggested dangerous imprudence to Lady Russell. Anne Elliot had been 'persuaded to believe the engagement a wrong thing—indiscreet, improper, hardly capable of success, and not deserving it' (Chapter 4). The moral reasoning here combines two principles: one is calculation of likely outcome, which is rated unfavourably; the other is a judgment of absolute worth. Presumably, the engagement does not deserve to succeed because it is 'indiscreet' and 'improper'. These are vague words: perhaps the first of them refers to the possible outcome of Frederick's hopes: it is 'indiscreet' because he is not thought likely to succeed in his profession. 'Improper', on the other hand, may carry suggestions of the disparity in social position between the pair. In rejecting him, Anne tried to act for what she saw as Frederick's good, though he did not agree with this assessment. The forces that prompted Anne to break her engagement are significant: they consist of external pressures based on a calculation of what might happen, and of her acceptance that the calculation is correct and should be accepted by her. She does not think it right to consult her own interest or define it for herself: on the contrary, she thinks self-denial is virtuous in itself. For Anne the result of her decision has been suffering and a contraction of her enjoyment of life.

The story of this past episode is related with sober sympathy; Anne has not met any other young man attractive enough to marry, and she now looks destined for an unfulfilled spinsterhood. She believes she has made a sacrifice which produced immediate unhappiness, believing it would be for the eventual good of Frederick. But Frederick has been successful and is now wealthy; he is also unmarried. Through this sad experience Anne has come to value romantic love because it implies a confidence in the future

n is healthier than the pessimism produced by the calcuations of pru-
ice. (Compare, in *Emma*, Frank Churchill's 'disposition to hope for
good'. ) Anne's self-inflicted wound, however, has never healed, though
no one knows of the pain it still causes.

When Sir Walter meets the Admiral, agreement is soon reached. Sir
Walter and Elizabeth move to Bath, while Anne remains behind to help her
sister Mary—a selfish, complaining woman, given to illness—before
travelling to Bath with Lady Russell to join the others. The only danger in
these arrangements is that Mrs Clay is to accompany Elizabeth and Sir
Walter to Bath. When Anne suggests that this young, obsequious woman
may not be a proper companion for Sir Walter, Elizabeth rejects her view:
after all, Mrs Clay has freckles! As the party leaves for Bath, the narrator
shows how Sir Walter deceives himself about his relationships with others:

> The party drove off in very good spirit; Sir Walter prepared with conde-
> scending bows for all the afflicted tenantry and cottagers who might
> have had a hint to show themselves. (*Chapter 5*)

Sir Walter is ready to be admired, and to acknowledge the supporters of the
pyramid of power on which he stands: he does not appear to care whether
their emotion at his departure is genuine or to ask what has prompted it.
Jane Austen's description of the scene binds its truth and falsehood into a
single clause, which compels us to judge Sir Walter as either too much of a
fool to understand what is happening or too self-deluded to care that he is
taking part in an elaborate social charade, which no honest man could fail
to find shoddy.

When Anne moves to Uppercross Cottage to be with her sister, Mary,
and her family, we soon see that Mary shares Sir Walter's capacity for self-
deception. Mary Musgrove has not sunk to the state of permanent lassitude
enjoyed by Lady Bertram of *Mansfield Park*, but she shares much of her
habitual need for support. She sees the world from a selfishly limited point
of view, which is unreasonable and inconsistent. She complains of being
neglected by her husband and his relatives, of Anne's tardiness in coming
to see her, of her lack of interest in her affairs. Mary has her father's consciousness of social distinction, but she has no superiority of person or
character to justify it. The Musgrove family, to whom she is related by
marriage, have no such pretensions. Mrs and Mrs Musgrove, who live at
Uppercross House, are homely and good-tempered; her sisters-in-law,
Henrietta and Louisa, are high-spirited and popular. Anne does not envy,
or wish to emulate, them, but she can see that they enjoy themselves and
are friendly to one another in a way she has never been with her own sisters.

Being at Uppercross is for Anne 'another lesson . . . in the art of knowing our own nothingness beyond our own circle' (Chapter 6). She sees all
the advantages of conforming to the habits of her new associates, who are
not unpleasant, even if they are not sympathetic. She sees that her sister

and brother-in-law are happy enough, although they differ too much in character to support and enhance one another. She is the recipient of the complaints of two households about each other's capacities and attitudes. Anne does what she can to mediate and reconcile, and to improve the management of Mary's household and children. However imperfect the household of Mary's parents-in-law might be, in good-breeding and in orderliness, Anne cannot help contrasting its warmth and liveliness with the coldness and formality of her own experience of home.

How difficult it is to eliminate personal bias is illustrated when Anne meets Mrs Croft for the first time. She is able to talk confidently to her since she believes that Mrs Croft does not associate her with her brother. Suddenly Mrs Croft disconcerts her by referring to her friendship with him. It soon appears they are talking at cross-purposes: Mrs Croft is referring to her brother, the clergyman, while Anne is thinking of her former sweetheart. Soon it becomes known that Captain Wentworth has returned to England and is likely to be asked to Uppercross, because he had once been kind to a now dead son, still mourned by Mrs Musgrove, even although he was thought to be of little use to anyone while he was alive.

If there is warmth and supportiveness at the Great House, conditions at Uppercross Cottage are less favourable. The accident sustained by one of the children provides an insight into the essentially selfish attitude of Charles and Mary Musgrove as their concern for their son's health is gradually overlaid by their curiosity to see Captain Wentworth, whose arrival has caused some excitement at the Great House. Charles Musgrove explains to his wife how little use he can be in looking after the little boy. Mary complains about his proposed desertion of them and argues that the feelings of a mother make her particularly unsuited to be a nurse. Mary does not appear to have the feelings Anne would expect of a mother: she is more apt to scold than to comfort. She is happy to accept Anne's offer to remain behind to look after the child, while she and her husband dine with Captain Wentworth. While the parents go off to be happy, 'however oddly constructed such happiness might seem', Anne, who cannot be persuaded to join them later, is left to speculate about Captain Wentworth and his attitudes to her.

A very large part of the interest of *Persuasion* lies in Jane Austen's exploration of the impenetrability of the intentions of others. Anne knows how she would have behaved, if she had been a man who wanted to renew an old acquaintance. She can only assume Captain Wentworth wants to avoid her. In fact his behaviour is ambiguous: he has let it be known that he remembers Anne, and he makes a point of having his first visit clearly signalled in advance. Their first brief meeting affects her powerfully but she tries to remind herself how long a time has passed since she has seen him. Mary's report of his opinion that she was 'altered beyond his knowledge' (Chapter 7) helps to calm Anne by suggesting she has no grounds for hope.

Despite the fact that their relationship is now merely formal, Anne cannot forget the sense of closeness they once shared. As we follow the apparently aimless conversation which takes place after dinner at Uppercross House, we notice that Jane Austen keeps returning to the theme of the discrepancy to be found between reason and sentiment: Frederick's response of something like contempt for Mrs Musgrove's mourning for her son is rational, but he suppresses this reaction, in favour of a more human sympathy. Human reaction, of course, need not be sympathetic. It is rational to hold that a middle-aged woman who is no longer attractive, and who is neither eloquent nor intelligent has a perfect right to grieve for her talentless son, but onlookers may also feel tempted to laugh. If there is strife between reason and sentiment, there is no easy way of judging which is right. Captain Wentworth is willing to convey Mrs Harville and her family by ship to Plymouth, because Harville is his friend, though reason tells him that a ship is no place for women. The Crofts, who are Anne's best model for a happy marriage, believe he will feel differently when he is married. Anne and the reader are left to wonder whether there remains any lingering sentiment that will turn Frederick's thoughts to her.

In the eyes of his relatives and friends there can be no goal except marriage for a man like Captain Wentworth who is young, handsome, rich and single. Henrietta and Louisa Musgrove, and some vaguely specified female cousins, called Hayter, are obvious contenders for his favour. Jane Austen now sets up an elimination contest between the available women. First, Charles Hayter, a young clergyman absent at the time of Wentworth's arrival, appears to claim Henrietta, with whom he has had an understanding. Whereas the older Musgroves, who have been established as unpretentious representatives of traditional English ways, leave such matters to their daughters' choosing, the younger Musgroves at Uppercross Cottage, think that wealth and honours are the main reasons for marriage. Mary Musgrove, in particular, looks down on Charles Hayter, a mere curate, while her husband, more sympathetically disposed to his cousin, thinks that Frederick should marry Louisa.

In such a context of changing relationships, Jane Austen sets an unexpected personal encounter between Wentworth and Anne at Uppercross Cottage. Nothing much happens, but Jane Austen is now adept at using body-posture to indicate states of internal emotional tension. When they meet unexpectedly, Wentworth turns to the window; Anne would leave, but is detained by one of the children. They are joined by Hayter who reads a newspaper to avoid contact with his rival. When Wentworth steps forward to remove a second child who has climbed on Anne's back, her feelings are confused. Through the child a current of feeling has been restored, but neither has spoken. Has Frederick deliberately avoided speaking? Anne is left to sort out disordered feelings which cannot easily be harmonised with any reasonable interpretation of Frederick's intention.

Using her own experience, Anne soon concludes that there is no question of love between Wentworth and either of the girls. They admire him: he, unwisely, is willing to accept their admiration. Charles Hayter's withdrawal from Uppercross gives rise to much speculation about his relationship with Henrietta. Whatever the reason for his absence, it appears to prompt the walk which Henrietta and Louisa take (in Chapter 10 of the first volume). Anne now sees some of the disadvantages of the Musgrove's family's sociability. The girls feel compelled to communicate their plan to take a walk; Mary feels compelled to join them; Anne goes too, so that she can keep Mary from interfering; and Charles and Wentworth also join them. Anne fixes her attention on 'the last smiles of the year upon the tawny leaves and withering hedges' — appropriate objects for her own autumnal musings — but cannot help overhearing the talk between Wentworth and the girls. Louisa's praise of the Crofts's married happiness strikes a chord with the Captain, producing a silence which chills Anne, bringing to her mind verses which speak of departed hopes. Of course, we think of Anne herself. But Jane Austen uses the farmland they are passing through to suggest the possibility of another spring. Now they have come — but surely not by chance — to the farm where the Hayters live. Louisa takes the lead in urging Henrietta to call on her cousins: Mary declines to join them, uttering a disparaging remark about the Hayters that draws a contemptuous glance from Frederick Wentworth. Louisa detaches Wentworth from the group and Mary follows them jealously, vainly attempting to conceal her anxiety to keep them under her eye.

We may be reminded of the scene at Sotherton in *Mansfield Park* where the two Bertram girls jostle for the attention of Henry Crawford. Louisa, triumphant for the moment, tells Wentworth how she has persuaded Henrietta to visit Hayter and just how much persuasion she required. Wentworth eloquently praises her firmness of character, suggesting that this is the first of virtues. The distinction between firmness and obstinacy is not made here, though it will be crucial to the later development of Louisa's character. Overhearing their conversation, Anne is mortified when Louisa tells Wentworth that Anne had been Charles Musgrove's first choice as a wife but that Anne had been persuaded to refuse him. Once again, Anne is agitated not only by this further evidence of her indecisiveness and dependence on others but by the irrational hopes aroused by any sign of Frederick's interest in her.

And yet, before the walk is over, Anne is given further evidence of his interest in her, when, seeing she is tired, he virtually compels her to accept a seat in the Admiral's gig which happens to be passing. Anne's conclusion about his feelings for her is that

He could not forgive her, — but he could not be unfeeling. Though condemning her for the past, and considering it with high and unjust resentment, though perfectly careless of her, and though becoming attached to another, still he could not see her suffer, without the desire of giving her relief. It was a remainder of former sentiment; it was an impulse of pure, though unacknowledged friendship; it was a proof of his own warm and amiable heart . . . (*Chapter 10*)

Anne's assessment of his state of mind, which may be a just evaluation of Frederick's conscious intention, falls neatly into two parts. The first two sentences carry her reasoned judgment, the conclusion preceding her analysis of what she believes he feels. The third sentence is divided into three parts, each of which carries a strong, unreasoning hope, in which insight into Wentworth's real nature is compounded with her own desire that he should love her. It is a little crescendo of affection, clear evidence of her own undiminished love.

Jane Austen develops apparently casual words and actions into significant signs of more permanent aspects of her characters: Anne's interest in nature and the literature associated with it points both to the refinement of her sensibility and to her proneness to despondency. She uses the poetry she remembers as a screen to protect her from the pain caused by Wentworth and Louisa's budding friendship. But with another part of her mind she misses nothing of their conversation or of the direction in which their walk is taking them. It is a casual, but subtle, example of the mind's capacity for self-division, its ability to shut out painful information and yet be alert to everything that might interest it. Wentworth's playful use of a hazel-nut to represent the firm mind he hopes Louisa will always possess serves also as an emblem for Anne herself, representing the triumph of maturity over the storms of autumn, an impression strengthened by the earlier association of Anne with autumnal imagery. The point is that Anne's own despondency is balanced by Jane Austen's use of the same imagery to suggest endurance and hope, although to Anne herself it had suggested decay and death. The Crofts are used to suggest a marriage which is a happy partnership. Anne's association with them in the gig (in a chapter where the grouping of the characters has been significant) is a final example of the economy with which telling symbolic use is made of chance association.

When Lady Russell returns to Kellynch, new possibilities are opened up. Anne is to join her there, thus possibly bringing her closer to Frederick, unless he continues his visits to Uppercross. But a quite new development takes place: Frederick learns that his friend Captain Harville is living nearby at Lyme. Louisa, whose decisiveness Frederick has commended, decides that all six should visit him. There they meet Captain and Mrs Harville and Captain Benwick, who had been engaged to Captain Harville's sister, who has recently died. Benwick, a rather introverted man with literary tastes, hopes to recover from his loss by living quietly with the Harvilles. Anne finds herself drawn to Captain Benwick, because of her own experience of loss and her interest in reading. He is, in fact, so deeply interested in poetry, which seems to reflect the depth of his own feelings, that Anne recommends 'a larger allowance of prose in his daily study' (Chapter 11). Here, as elsewhere, Jane Austen dwells on the meeting-point between feeling and reason. Penetrating questions about feeling lie below the surface of the narrative: what function does it serve in our lives? What attention should be paid to it? Is it dangerous, and, if so, what resources do we have to preserve us from its inroads. If *Persuasion* is Jane Austen's most sympathetic study of the place of feeling in human life, Captain Benwick is a reminder of the dangers of it in excess.

The final chapter of Volume One (Chapter 12) produces the astonishing climax of Louisa Musgrove's memorable fall as she obstinately jumps from some steps on the Cobb. Only Anne has the presence of mind to send Benwick for a doctor. Charles and Frederick look to her for advice, and the Harvilles give a further demonstration of their practical good sense by taking Louisa into their house. Mary's characteristic insistence on her right to look after her sister (in spite of her incompetence to do so) means that Henrietta, Wentworth and Anne return to Uppercross in the chaise, but Wentworth's attention is for Henrietta. Only once does he speak to Anne directly, but his way of asking for advice gives her great pleasure — 'as a proof of friendship, and of deference for her judgment.' Although he returns to Lyme — and Louisa — immediately, Anne knows he respects her.

## Volume Two (*Chapters 13–25*)

The second volume of the novel marks a change of direction. Anne's return to Lady Russell at Kellynch Lodge alters the focus of her attention. Now, she is expected to think of her father and sister in Bath, though her feelings are still enmeshed with her friends at Uppercross and Lyme. Before Anne leaves for Kellynch, she is able to experience the ache of her own loneliness at Uppercross, since she has persuaded the rest of the Musgrove family to go to Lyme, where all the work of looking after Louisa is being done by Mrs Harville. Anne leaves with regret:

> Scenes had passed in Uppercross, which made it precious. It stood the record of many sensations of pain, once severe, but now softened; and of some instances of relenting feeling, some breathings of friendship and reconciliation, which could never be looked for again . . .
> (*Chapter 13*)

These are the characteristic autumnal musings which we associate with Anne Elliot, the distinctive notes of her inner world of feeling, to which we are given access in a fuller and more poignant way than to the consciousness

of any other of Jane Austen's heroines. But although this mood predomi-
nates, there are more hopeful signs: Lady Russell compliments her on her
looks; perhaps she may 'be blessed with a second spring of youth and
beauty' (Chapter 13). At the deepest level of this novel, underlying its discussions of reason and feeling, and of the limitations of our knowledge of
others, there is a theme of renewal, perfectly natural in the cycle of the
seasons, more wayward and mysterious in the course of human life.

News of Louisa comes from Charles and Mary Musgrove, though
Mary's account of her stay at Lyme shows that her main concern has been
for herself. They have news, too, of Captain Benwick, whom Mary dis-
likes for his bookishness and his lack of attention to herself. Charles
expects him to visit Kellynch because of his interest in Anne; Mary disagrees, but it is not clear whether she thinks he is not interested in Anne or
expects everyone's interest to be focused upon herself. Benwick, however,
does not come: he is one of Anne's 'phantom' suitors, a false trail laid by
Jane Austen to mislead the unwary reader. The other is Mr Elliot, whom
they are to meet when they move to Bath, after Jane Austen has made a
pointed comparison between the noisy cheerfulness of a family Christmas
at Uppercross and the fashionable bustle of Bath. Though Anne cannot
wholly enter into the 'high revel' of the former situation, she does not hesitate to dislike the latter.

Sir Walter and Elizabeth, who are more cordial than Anne expected,
have little time for news of Kellynch and Uppercross. As Jane Austen has
noted before, human beings are anxious to talk about themselves. They
seem to have no idea how diminished their state of life is, now that Sir Walter has abandoned his duties as a landowner. Mr Elliot, whom Anne met
briefly at Lyme, has rather strangely sought his relatives' acquaintance,
despite the lengthy breach between them. Sir Walter imagines his cousin
now values the attention of the head of the family. Anne assumes that a
former liking for Elizabeth is the reason, though she wonders if Mr Elliot
will be prompted to propose on a closer acquaintance with Elizabeth's
character. Anne's thoughts on these matters are swamped by Sir Walter's
own impressions, which are mainly concerned with appearance and manner. Jane Austen makes a point of stressing the essentially narcissistic elements in Sir Walter's evaluation of his world: no one survives his critical
scrutiny apart from himself and a select few of whom he approves.

When Mr Elliot appears at Sir Walter's house in Camden Place — Jane
Austen is keenly aware of the precise social nuance which Bath addresses
carry — he recognises Anne. While she is willing to compare him, not
unfavourably, to Captain Wentworth in appearance and manner, it is to
Lady Russell she compares him in mental ability and conversational
power. The judgment is not disparaging — his conversation is the product
of 'a sensible, discerning mind' — but it is a limiting one. In the chapter that
follows, Jane Austen makes a point of dissociating Anne from some of the

attitudes of the two people of whom she approves in many ways, and who certainly represent the average opinion of right-thinking people.

The most significant divergence between Anne and her two friends is on the question of rank. The arrival of the Dowager Viscountess Dalrymple, who is a distant relative of the Elliots, excites Sir Walter's self-importance (Chapter 16). Mr Elliot and Lady Russell support his desire to make her acquaintance on the grounds that Lady Dalrymple and her daughter are worth knowing and have their values 'as those who would collect good company around them'. Anne's idea of good company is 'the company of clever, well-informed people, who have a great deal of conversation', but for Mr Elliot, 'rank is rank'; all that matters is that they should enjoy 'all the credit and dignity which ought to belong to Sir Walter Elliot'.

In contrast to Sir Walter's cultivation of his social superiors, Anne is renewing her acquaintance with an old school friend, who had comforted her when she was in mourning for her mother. Now Anne is 'an elegant little woman of seven and twenty, with every beauty excepting bloom, and with manners as consciously right as they were invariably gentle'; Mrs Smith is a crippled widow in reduced circumstances. She has a claim to being included in Anne's definition of good company, since she is cheerful, willing to talk and possessed of good sense. In spite of deprivation and isolation, she is not often depressed. She is far from being the model of stoic acceptance, which often appears to be Anne's aim for herself. Like the Crofts and the Harvilles and the elder Musgroves, Mrs Smith has gifts which have nothing to do with rank, or even with ability, but are a natural endowment of temperament and spirit. But the flight from self to others, from despondency to cheerfulness, from evil to good can be learned as a virtue, if it is not possessed by nature. A generous capacity for thinking of the good of others is necessary for authorial approval in this novel.

When Anne's friendship with Mrs Smith becomes known, the reaction of her father and sister is predictably snobbish. Sir Walter dwells with heavy sarcasm on Mrs Smith's common name and unfashionable address. His prejudice against her is only equalled by his unreasoning partiality for Mrs Clay. Jane Austen is careful to exonerate Lady Russell and Mr Elliot from this ignorant and rather brutal attack on Anne's generous feelings. Lady Russell takes Anne to visit Mrs Smith in her carriage; Mr Elliot praises her compassion. Lady Russell clearly believes Mr Elliot may be interested in Anne and that she would do well to take her late mother's place as mistress of Kellynch Hall. The mention of her mother is almost enough to sway Anne's mind in Mr Elliot's favour, but now she is more cautious of Lady Russell's advice. Despite Mr Elliot's manner, she suspects there are things in his past with which she would be unhappy. It is his lack of openness — just the quality she admires in the naval officers she has come to know — which she most deplores. It is as if, in Anne Elliot, Jane Austen has reconciled those opposed character-types — the enthusiastic and impulsive, on the one hand, and the scrupulous adherent of truth and duty, on the other—which in her earlier novels she has felt forced to choose between. Generosity and warmth of spirit are now admitted to the canon of virtues and given a first place among them. Mr Elliot is agreeable, well-mannered, sensible and compliant, but these are virtues which Anne does not find sufficient for the man she wants to marry.

News of Anne's friends at Uppercross arrives in a letter from Mary, delivered through the Crofts who have arrived in Bath. Its complaints about the ill-usage she has suffered are characteristic, but the letter contains one surprising piece of news: Captain Benwick has become engaged to Louisa Musgrove. Mere proximity has brought this ill-assorted couple together, and Anne muses on the accident which has settled Louisa's destiny. She can now think of Wentworth as 'unshackled and free' and is almost ashamed to acknowledge the feelings of 'senseless joy' which pervade her.

The renewal of Anne's acquaintance with Wentworth is preceded by an incident in which she is obliged to perform a social quadrille with her sister, Mrs Clay and Mr Elliot about who is to escape the rain in Lady Dalrymple's barouche and who is to walk home with the gentleman. In the light of subsequent events, Mrs Clay's dispute with Anne for the privilege of walking may be the first hint of her later association with Mr Elliot. On a first reading, it simply displays her apparent need to appear humble.

When Anne sees Wentworth from the door of the shop where they are sheltering, she dismisses her companions from her mind. She hurries out, ostensibly to see if the rain has stopped, in reality to see where Wentworth is going. Anne's state of half-conscious self-deception is presented sympathetically; for a moment she is allowed to defy the internal censors which would forbid her to use the weather to disguise an impulse of sexual curiosity. (Isabella Thorpe in *Northanger Abbey* would have practised such a deception brazenly and would have been sharply condemned for it by her creator.) When they meet, what interests Jane Austen is their sense of mutual awareness: Anne's consciousness mirrors Wentworth's, noticing every nuance of his embarrassment and his inability to disguise it from her. She is also aware of the exchange of feeling between Wentworth and her sister, each knowing the other, but the lady refusing to acknowledge the relationship which the man is willing to renew. In such passages, Jane Austen traces these currents of feeling with a new freedom, unencumbered by too strict a regard for what her characters ought to feel. Of course, the public surface of these inner agitations is constrained by a social etiquette which leaves little to individual initiative: Captain Wentworth offers his umbrella; Anne declines; Mr Elliot bears her off on his arm.

Captain Wentworth's companions draw an easy conclusion about the relationship between Anne and her cousin: Jane Austen makes a point of reminding us how Wentworth had noticed Elliot's admiring glance at Anne on their first chance meeting. But Anne can scarcely attend to Mr Elliot, her mind is so full of Wentworth. She begins to suffer an intolerable tension of uncertainty about Wentworth. She is 'sick of knowing nothing, and fancying herself stronger because her strength was not tried' (Chapter 19): she needs the test of a personal encounter with him so that she can replace her inner fantasies with certain knowledge, and discover in the process how far she can bear the reality of her relationship with him.

Her opportunity comes at a concert that evening. Jane Austen leaves us in no doubt about the effort required for Anne to gain, and keep, Wentworth's attention. Once more, she displays her command of the staging of such scenes: in the background Sir Walter and Elizabeth's presence can be felt, but Anne, with her back to them, can be guided by her own sense of what to do. The bare recognition which Wentworth receives from her relatives is the first step in his rehabilitation. When Anne speaks to him, their conversation is circumspect: only at its edges are there hints that the Musgroves are treating the marriage of their daughter with a generosity Sir Walter did not show to Anne. Jane Austen makes much of the glances, blushes and hesitations which punctuate their talk. Wentworth's emphatic words about faithfulness in love are almost dispersed in the noise of the room and by the stress of his emotion, but Anne loses none of them. She cannot respond directly to what he says about constancy in love, though she can express the pleasure her visit to Lyme has given her. At least to herself it is clear that what pleased her was his company.

Such moments of guarded personal intercourse are subordinated to the demands of the outer world: on Lady Dalrymple's entrance, the groups reform. Anne is left to reflect on what has happened, to conclude that Wentworth's behaviour amounts to an admission that he still loves her. Now her happiness depends on re-establishing contact with him—even a meeting of eyes would be something. When the concert begins, she finds herself beside Mr Elliot whose mysterious remarks about having heard of her before he came to Bath cause her disquiet. At the interval, she keeps her seat, hoping Wentworth will come to her. She moves to the end of the row, and catches his eye. This time his approach is more reluctant: Jane Austen tracks his movements as he considers whether he should sit with Anne. Mr Elliot intervenes with a question about the concert, and Wentworth departs abruptly with a phrase that suggests he is jealous.

The final stage of the novel begins in romance and continues in melodrama. Anne is a woman in love, eternally in love—whether she marries him or not—with Captain Wentworth. Anne has no reason to think badly of Mr Elliot; she is even grateful to him for his admiration. But if Mr Elliot has played a part in the novel by helping to re-kindle Wentworth's interest in Anne, it is now time for him to be eliminated as a serious contender for her. Jane Austen falls back on disclosure, one of her favourite narrative devices, using it with more melodrama than subtlety.

The unmasking of Mr Elliot as a self-centred opportunist has not been unprepared for. In an earlier chapter (Chapter 3, Volume Two) Anne wonders why he is now anxious to renew his severed relationship with the Elliot family. There has also been the puzzle of his having prior knowledge of Anne's character. It is Anne's impoverished friend, Mrs Smith, who now discloses his history, after she has discovered that Anne and Mr Elliot are not to marry. Now she is willing to tell the truth she was equally willing to conceal:

> 'Mr Elliot is a man without heart or conscience; a designing, wary, cold-blooded being, who thinks only of himself; who, for his own interest or ease, would be guilty of any cruelty, or any treachery, that could be perpetrated without risk of his general character. He has no feeling for others. Those whom he has been the chief cause of leading into ruin, he can neglect and desert without the smallest compunction. He is totally beyond the reach of any sentiment of justice or compassion. Oh! he is black at heart, hollow and black!' (*Chapter 21*)

This is surely the language of melodrama, though Mrs Smith supports her accusations by an account of her own experience of him. It is plausible that Mr Elliot has chosen to marry a girl with money rather than fall in with Sir Walter's scheme of marrying his eldest daughter. It is perhaps less plausible that he had quite such contempt for the baronetcy he was to inherit and the family of which he was a member. Luckily—but perhaps a little surprisingly—Mrs Smith has preserved a letter written over a decade before, which expressed his contempt for Sir Walter and Kellynch Hall. Now, it seems, his opinions have changed: whereas in 1803, he could regard Sir Walter's possible re-marriage with unconcern, he is now extremely anxious to thwart the designs of Mrs Clay. Despite the care which Jane Austen has taken to provide the missing facts of Mr Elliot's history, it is difficult to regard this part of the narrative as other than an awful warning of the fate which might have befallen Anne. Wickedness on this scale seems a less likely feature of the world Jane Austen has created than folly: like General Tilney in *Northanger Abbey*, Mr Elliot (in Mrs Smith's account of him) has some of the characteristics of the villains of romantic fiction.

Two versions remain of how Jane Austen thought the novel might end: in the first, two chapters only followed Mrs Smith's revelation. In the first of them, Anne Elliot meets Admiral Croft by chance just outside his lodgings. Assuming that she is on her way to visit his wife, he invites her in. There she finds herself alone with Wentworth who has been deputed to explain that the Admiral is willing to give up Kellynch Hall to Anne and Mr Elliot in the event of their marriage. Anne is able to say that they are not engaged and the way is left clear for Wentworth to declare his own love.

The second ending is much more elaborate: in place of the penultimate chapter of the novel, Jane Austen wrote two substantial chapters, postponing the reconciliation and bringing to Bath some of the characters, introduced at Uppercross and Lyme, who have had no part to play in the second volume of the novel. This provides an opportunity for a final contrast to be made between the coldness of Anne's family and the boisterous warmth of the Musgroves, always excepting Mary Musgrove, who is never able to throw off the self-regarding demeanour she has inherited from her father. The re-written tenth chapter (Chapter 22) of the second volume begins with Anne's enlightened view of Mr Elliot. He and Mrs Clay are now seen as a comparable pair of hypocrites whose secret aim is to destroy the peace of mind of Sir Walter and Elizabeth. Anne means to visit Lady Russell to tell her what she has learned from Mrs Smith but she is prevented from doing so by the arrival of Mary and Charles Musgrove. They have come to Bath with a selection of their friends from Uppercross, chosen, perhaps, because they offer fewest complications for the closing stage of the novel: Henrietta is there, but not Louisa; Captain Harville, but not Captain Benwick. While Mary is admiring her father's drawing-rooms, Anne discovers that Henrietta is now able to marry Charles Hayter and Louisa will soon marry Captain Benwick. It is an opportunity for Charles and Anne to agree about the generosity of the elder Musgroves and for Charles to rescue the reputation of Benwick from the imputation of spinelessness. Even if she is not able to share the joyfulness of the Musgrove family, Anne is able to feel glad for them.

It is within the 'heartiness' and 'warmth' of the Musgrove rooms at the White Hart hotel that Anne meets Captain Wentworth once more, but, even if he is not present, Mr Elliot still constitutes a barrier between them. Jane Austen has thickened her plot by allowing Mary to spot Mr Elliot talking to Mrs Clay at a corner of a street, although he is supposed to be out of town for a day or two. Officiously, she asks Anne for confirmation, implying that Anne has special knowledge of his movements. It is the first of two opportunities which Anne has to distance herself from Mr Elliot and her family: in making the point clear, she is rewarded, first, by a glance from Wentworth, then by his approaching her. There is time for only a brief sentence before they are interrupted, but it is enough that Wentworth has referred to the time of their earlier acquaintance.

In the second of the two additional chapters (Chapter 23), Anne pays another visit to the White Hart hotel. While Wentworth writes a letter in the corner of the room, Anne listens first to a conversation between Mrs Croft and Musgrove about the uncertainties of marriage for young people. But they do not imitate Lady Russell in recommending patience and prudence. Mrs Croft believes it is better for young people to marry on a small income and struggle with their early difficulties, while Mrs Musgrove describes the anxious, but open, discussions which went on between parents and children before Henrietta's wedding was decided upon. This affectionate consideration contrasts with the prudent coldness Anne and Wentworth experienced. Captain Harville introduces a second, more painful, topic. Benwick's engagement to Louisa implies a breach of faith with the memory of Harville's sister. Do women have longer memories than men? Or are their feelings stronger? Despite Captain Benwick's fondness for poetry, he has been able to forget his dead sweetheart more quickly than seems decent. For the first time in her novels, Jane Austen explicitly contrasts the social conditions of men and women, which affect the character of their emotional lives. Anne says to Harville:

> 'We certainly do not forget you, so soon as you forget us. It is, perhaps, our fate rather than our merit . . . We live at home, quiet, confined, and our feelings prey upon us. You are forced on exertion. You have always a profession, pursuits, business of some sort or other, to take you back into the world immediately, and continual occupation and change soon weakens impression.' (*Chapter 23*)

Although Anne does not believe it is a defect to remember, there is a wistfulness about her reference to the inactivity which leaves women a prey to their feelings. Men's feelings may be more violent but they are less robust. Anne does not deny that a man—a sailor, perhaps—who is separated from his wife and family, will yearn to see them again. What she does claim is that women treasure the memory of their loved ones, even when they are gone. It is a sentiment she expresses with a deeply-felt eloquence, which springs from the poignancy of her own faithful love for Wentworth. Although it is obvious that Wentworth has overheard what has been said, Anne is puzzled by his haste to leave her, but in a moment he is back when the room is clear enough for him to give her a letter without being observed. It contains a declaration of his own constancy, and a final appeal: 'A word, a look will be enough to decide whether I enter your father's house this evening, or never.'

There is no attempt to underestimate the effect this letter has upon Anne's sensibility; the entrance of the other members of the party gives her no time to deal with her feelings. Anxiety, almost of a neurotic kind, begins to attack her: weak as she is, she must walk home, in case she might meet Wentworth. Perhaps there has been a misunderstanding about his invitation to her father's; if she does not speak to him before evening he may not come. Anne fears that the happiness, so long denied her, will still somehow slip away. But Wentworth overtakes her as she walks home with Charles:

> He joined them; but, as if irresolute whether to join or to pass on, said nothing—only looked. Anne could command herself enough to receive that look, and not repulsively. The cheeks which had been pale now glowed, and the movements which had hesitated were decided. He walked by her side. (*Chapter 23*)

Readers must decide for themselves whether these actions can be understood only by a vigorous act of historical imagination or whether such shy, scarcely perceptible, movements can still be accepted as the outward signs of an inward affection. Fuller explanations follow. Left on their own, the lovers have time to make a detailed examination of their more recent conduct: all their feelings, words, looks and actions are gradually made intelligible as manifestations of jealousy or love. As readers, we have been more in touch than Wentworth with Anne's weakness and timidity, but these have stemmed from a self-mistrust produced by the consciousness of past mistakes. It is difficult in the concluding radiant passages describing the reconciliation of the lovers not to be reminded of the ancient image of the elm and the vine, symbols of the differing qualities men and women were thought to bring to married love, the woman beautiful and fruitful, the man strong and supportive. However unfashionable now, these images seem appropriate to a relationship in which Anne and Wentworth are renewed.

Although the new material which Jane Austen has introduced into the ending of the novel reintegrates Anne with the happy community of the lesser gentry of Uppercross and the naval officers and their wives, the core of *Persuasion* consists of its account of Anne's inner life. If it reminds us in part of a folk-tale, it is because it tells of a semi-miraculous renewal of life, of a recovery of the past, of a second chance to do well what was ill-done before. The advice not to marry, given her by Lady Russell, may or may not have been right, but she was right to take it because it was her duty to do so. So Anne reasons, but we may think that the novel as a whole points to a concept of morality not rooted in abstract notions of duty but one open to feeling and desire, and more in touch with the needs of the self and the complexities of particular moments of choice. What Anne may have most distinctly learned are the dangers of neglecting to choose for oneself, of curbing the active impulse of the affections in order to conform with the maxims of a timid society.

Anne Elliot is, of course, another of Jane Austen's instructional models, less forbidding than Fanny Price, because older, less sure of herself, more certain of the painful consequences of continuing to love a man one has lost. She exemplifies the disciplined self, aware of the demands made on her by her emotions but strong enough to subject them to the superior demands of self respect. She is aware of the disadvantages of solitariness and the suffering caused by loneliness, but she would rather experience the rigours of these conditions than allow her unsatisfied ego to be an affliction to others. But she also knows that it is only through others, and through the freely exchanged affections of social life, that the self can be fulfilled.

# Suggestions for further reading

## The texts

The standard edition of Jane Austen's novels is by R.W. Chapman, 6 volumes (Oxford University Press, Oxford, 1923–54, revised by Mary Lascelles, 1965–7). These volumes have prefaces, notes, appendices and indexes by R.W. Chapman: later re-prints have additional notes by Mary Lascelles. Volume 6, which includes the early works, *Lady Susan*, *The Watsons* and *Sanditon*, has additional notes by B.C. Southam (1969). Other editions can be found in the Oxford English Novels series, with introductions, notes and bibliographies. Paperback editions with introductions and notes have been published by Penguin Books, by The New American Library of World Literature Inc. (as Signet Classics) and by Pan Books Ltd (as Pan Classics).

## Biography and letters

AUSTEN-LEIGH, J.E.: *A Memoir of Jane Austen* (ed. R.W. Chapman) Clarendon Press, Oxford, 1926; 1967.

AUSTEN-LEIGH, W. and R.A.: *Jane Austen, Her Life and Letters*, Smith, Elder and Co., London, 1913.

CHAPMAN, R.W. (ED): *Jane Austen's Letters*, Oxford University Press, Oxford 1979.

CHAPMAN, R.W.: *Jane Austen, Facts and Problems*, Oxford University Press, Oxford 1948; 3rd edition, 1950.

HONAN, PARK: *Jane Austen. Her Life*, Weidenfeld and Nicolson, London, 1987.

JENKINS, ELIZABETH: *Jane Austen*, Gollancz, London, 1938.

## Background books

BRADBROOK, F.W.: *Jane Austen and her Predecessors*, Cambridge University Press, Cambridge, 1966.

CRAIK, W.A.: *Jane Austen in her Time*, Thomas Nelson and Sons Ltd, London 1969.

LASKI, MARGHANITA: *Jane Austen and her World*, Thames and Hudson, London, 1969.

PINION, F.B.: *A Jane Austen Companion*, Macmillan, London, 1973.

## General criticism

BABB, HOWARD S.: *Jane Austen's Novels: the fabric of dialogue*, Ohio State University Press, 1962.

BROWN, LLOYD W.: *Bits of Irony: narrative techniques in Jane Austen's fiction*, Louisiana University Press, Baton Rouge, 1973.

BUTLER, MARILYN: *Jane Austen and the War of Ideas*, Clarendon Press, Oxford, 1975.

CRAIK, W.A.: *Jane Austen: the six novels*, Methuen, London, 1965.

DUCKWORTH, A.M.: *The Improvement of the Estate: a study of Jane Austen's novels*, Johns Hopkins Press, Baltimore and London, 1971.

HALPERIN, JOHN (ED.).: *Jane Austen: Bicentenary Essays*, Cambridge University Press, Cambridge, 1975.

HARDY, BARBARA: *A Reading of Jane Austen*, Peter Owen, London,, 1975.

LASCELLES, MARY: *Jane Austen and her Art*, Clarendon Press, Oxford, 1939.

LITZ, A.W.: *Jane Austen: a study of her artistic development*, Chatto and Windus, London, 1965.

MUDRICK, M.: *Jane Austen: irony as defense and discovery*, Oxford University Press, London, 1952.

SOUTHAM, B.C.: *Jane Austen's Literary Manuscripts*, Oxford University Press, London, 1964.

SOUTHAM, B.C. (ED.): *Critical Essays on Jane Austen*, Routledge and Kegan Paul, London, 1968.

SOUTHAM, B.C. (ED.): *Jane Austen: the critical heritage*, Routledge and Kegan Paul, London, 1968.

WRIGHT, A.H.: *Jane Austen's Novels: a study in structure*, Chatto and Windus, London, 1953.

# Index

## PLACES REFERRED TO IN THE NOVELS

# The author of this Handbook

IAN MILLIGAN was educated at the University of Glasgow where he gained the degrees of MA and MED. After teaching in the Royal High School, Edinburgh, he became a lecturer in English at Moray House College of Education, Edinburgh. He now lectures in the Department of English Studies at the University of Stirling. He has published articles on education, on the teaching of literature and on nineteenth- and twentieth-century literature. He is the author of York Notes on Jane Austen's *Northanger Abbey*, Anthony Trollope's *Barchester Towers*, Richard Hughes's *A High Wind in Jamaica*, L.P. Hartley's *The Shrimp and the Anemone* and the York Handbook, *The English Novel*. He has also written the Macmillan Master Guide on *Howards End* by E.M. Forster and *The Novel in English: an Introduction*, Macmillan, London, 1983; 1987.